PEACE AND DEVELOPMENT
IN THE PACIFIC HEMISPHERE

PEACE AND DEVELOPMENT IN THE PACIFIC HEMISPHERE

JOHAN GALTUNG

University of Hawaii Institute for Peace
Honolulu

Library of Congress Cataloging-in-Publication Data

Galtung, Johan.
    Peace and development in the Pacific hemisphere / Johan Galtung.
       p.   cm.
    Bibliography: p.
    ISBN 0-8248-1262-X
    1. Pacific Area—Economic policy. 2. Peace. I. Title.
HC681.G34   1989
338.99—dc20   89-5042
                                                     CIP

Distributed by
University of Hawaii Press
Order Department
2840 Kolowalu Street
Honolulu, Hawaii 96822

CONTENTS

PREFACE

The University of Hawaii Institute for Peace asked me to give three lectures during the fall term of 1987 on the relation between peace and development. I found the topic so broad that I narrowed it a little to "Peace and Development in the Pacific Hemisphere." The lectures are offered here in a more permanent form, but essentially as originally presented. A few minor revisions have been made and notes are added. This book is also a publication of the Pacific Hemisphere Project directed by the author.

I would like to express my gratitude to the UHIP for inviting me to give the lectures, to the participants in the symposia for excellent comments, to Jon van Dyke and George Simson for their helpful advice, and to Carolyn DiPalma for a superb job preparing the manuscript.

CHAPTER 1

The Peace and Development Interfaces, and the "Swords into Plowshares" Hypothesis

What is the linkage between peace and development? It is not a simple relationship, and it also depends on what we mean by these two words. So we start with the meanings:

Peace I, narrow meaning: absence of war between states.

Peace II, broad meaning: absence of direct and structural violence between and within states, realizing survival + well-being + identity + freedom for all; in other words satisfaction of human needs, and in addition, ecological balance.

Development I, narrow meaning: economic growth, GNP, productivity, etc.

Development II, broad meaning: the satisfaction of human needs, the minimum people cannot do without, for all—survival + well-being + identity + freedom; and in addition, ecological balance.

Thus, taken in their broad meanings, peace = development. They are, in a sense, the same thing! So, why the difference in words? This is because the problem of peace in the narrow sense is what the rich countries are worried about, and the problem of development is what poor countries are worried about, with elites in both cases being concerned with the narrow meanings, and hungry people with the broad meanings. Hunger is the name for war in the Third World countries, says the famous Brazilian bishop, Helder Câmara.

The two terms derive from different concerns. In modern peace studies and development studies they are brought together—a reason why peace researchers also tend to study development, and vice versa. In traditional studies on international relations, people still stick to the narrow meanings that launch rich and poor countries on different agendas. The broad meanings of the two concepts bring them together in the same concern for peace = development = sustainable development (basic needs + ecological balance).

But if war and poverty, or rather misery, are of the same nature it should be possible to compare them. The concept of "structural violence" makes this possible. The idea is actually very simple. In a war, life is taken away from people. People are killed. But in misery, life is also taken away from people. They are not killed instantly or quickly by a bullet or a bomb; they are killed slowly, through diseases and malnutrition till they pass away, unnoticed except as statistics. We know people can live longer. We know it is possible today to live till one is, say, eighty years old; given the right health conditions, or even longer. But that means that a person who dies at the age of forty, whether through direct or structural violence, through war or misery, has half of his or her life taken away. An infant who dies as a result of lack of adequate food or poor hygiene has the whole life taken away. And that opens an important point. Misery is war, but not on everybody. It is war on poor people and poor countries, and especially on poor people in poor countries. It is a double class war, against low-class countries and low-class people. For we know today that this misery is avoidable. When it is not avoided it is because of social structures that have to be changed.

This idea, originally developed at the International Peace Research Institute in Oslo, was taken up by two U.S. researchers, Charles Zimmermann and Milton Leitenberg, in an article entitled "Hiroshima Lives On," published in *Mazingira*,[1] a magazine related to the United Nations Environment Program. They calculated the annual avoidable deaths among children by comparing the number of children who died in a country with the number who would have died had they had the health conditions of the United States, the reference country. They also did this for various age groups, and found that the youngest group, 0–4 years, made up 84% of the "excess deaths." Much of this was infant mortality. When they limited the study to the age group 1–5 years, they found that *the annual excess deaths from this group alone in the world amounted to deaths from 236 Hiroshima bombs.* They used the U.S. estimates of number of dead —68,000 for Hiroshima, 38,000 for Nagasaki—and calculated the average, 53,000. Recent Japanese estimates are 170,000 and 140,000, respectively (average 155,000)—100,000 higher! But regardless of that difference, these figures show the horrors of misery, and also how much more readily we get used to, and accept, misery than we accept war. Today at least 14 million children die every year, about 40,000 a day, before the age of 5—the phenomenon George Kent refers to as "The Silent Holocaust."

Let us now take the concepts "peace" and "development" in their more narrow, conventional meanings, as "absence of war" and "economic growth," and combine them with a third phenomenon, state-formation. The relation between the two then seems to be clearly negative: the more development, the less peace. In the famous work by Quincy Wright, *A Study of War,* very interesting data are given about how belligerence for economic or political gains against other societies relates to the "level of development."[2] If his data about nearly 500 societies are organized in a sequence from the most "primitive" to the most "civilized," there is no doubt that the most primitive are the most peaceful (with 0% belligerence, that is, engaging in only ritualistic warlike activities with a very low level of violence). The most civilized are clearly the most belligerent (95% of them). The primitive are nomadic societies: very simple social structure, the people living off nature, certainly with no economic growth—here the concept does not even make any sense—and the civilized are societies with fixed territory, a state organization, complex social structure, agriculture, and so on. "Civilization" and war seem to be related. It is among the societies whose people live very close to the state of nature that we find most peacefulness. Modern states based on military professionalism, killing in cold blood; on "death by distance" technology; general conscription—often coupled through an implicit contract with the state to a Bill of Rights and human rights in general and an ideology of nationalism—are the worst.

This is also seen very clearly in recent data about war after the Second World War, meaning after the capitulation of militarist Japan on 15 August 1945. According to the late Hungarian peace researcher István Kende,[3] there were 120 armed conflicts during the 32 years 1945 to 1976; 148 up to and including the Falkland/Malvinas war in 1982. He refers to them as "wars" because governmental forces were involved on at least one side, and as "local" since they were not world encompassing. The average number of wars on any given day in that period was 11.5. Only 5 of them took place in Europe, the remaining 115 in the Third World. North America as usual managed to keep wars outside that territory. About 80% of the war activity was clearly antiregime wars, with foreign participation. The intervention was by developed capitalist countries in 64 of the 120 wars, by socialist countries in 6 of them, and by Third World countries in 17 of them—particularly Cuba, Algeria, and Vietnam. And the major intervening powers were the United States, Great Britain, France, and Portugal—in that order. In other words, the most belligerent countries were also the most developed, with the exception of Portugal.

We know the reason and it is very simple. Their development was and is to a large extent based on colonial or neocolonial empires, and they wanted to keep them to protect their positions. The United States did not have colonies, but neo-colonies economically rather than politically and militarily dominated in the traditional sense. The war in Vietnam was not so much about Vietnam as it was about U.S. power and hegemony in general. And after the United States was beaten and had to withdraw, first in 1973, then in 1975, the dollar declined in value, as the pound had done earlier, and also the franc (not to mention the escudo). Rates of exchange are reflections not only of economic power, but also of military/political power.

Evidently war has been a means to development in the narrow sense. But peace has also been a means to development. The relation is complex, as mentioned at the beginning. A country can grow economically through imperialist, belligerent expansion—like Japan through the Sino-Japanese war 1894–95; the war against Russia 1904–05; the war against Korea 1910–11; the war against China, starting with what in Japan still is covered up as "the Manchurian incident," 1931; the extended war against China; and the Second World War with the effort to establish a real *dai-to-a kyoeiken* (the Greater East Asia Co-Prosperity Sphere). With territories like Formosa, Korea, and a good part of China, it was possible for Japan to have an external sector in her economy under total Japanese control, and to use it mainly for the development of Japan in the narrow sense. The war against Russia served to stave off competitors. But to be beaten in the Second World War, with tremendous destruction, also served development in the conventional sense for Japan: fixed capital destroyed had to be rebuilt. Lives destroyed could not be rebuilt, but that does not count in this narrow perspective. To rebuild defines a clear demand. The supply has to come forth; as a result production wheels start spinning as never before. Even to destroy other countries in a war and then repair the damage may stimulate development: "There is no business like reparation business." Economic growth stagnates when there is no effective demand; it picks up again when there is an effective demand. And that also applies to the wars of others. To be a supplier for the U.S. wars in Korea and Vietnam gave a tremendous boost to Japan's economic growth.

However, as mentioned, peace can also be good for development. The Romans used the word *pax* for peace, meaning *absentia belli,* the absence of war—within the Roman Empire. Trade is easier in times of peace, for obvious reasons. But the best is, perhaps, a combination of war and peace—"best," that is, for economic development. In one combination there would be war, in some place sufficiently far away not to involve oneself directly, and peace in the near surroundings to make it possible to supply war material to belligerents, or for them to use one's territory for bases. This formula has been used by many countries in East and Southeast Asia, not only by Japan.

Another formula would use time rather than space as the basic factor. First, have peace with growing production until there is overproduction, then a war to destroy fixed capital; then peace to rebuild, including rebuilding the production capacity; then again overproduction; then again war. And so on and on. These two formulas—the peace-war mix in space and in time—do not exclude each other.

Japan has, in fact, been using both, and extremely skillfully. In the diagram below, start with Japan '41–'45 and follow the arrows.

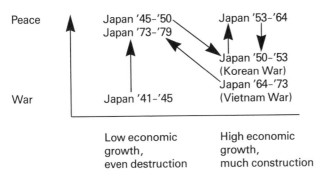

If there is something to this picture, the conclusion is obvious. If Japan should enter a really deep recession, a depression, one solution would be a new war sometime well into the 1990s, with Japan in any of the three possible roles: as conqueror, as conquered, or as supplier to either or both sides. The first role is, of course, excluded by the constitution (Article 9). The other two are not. It should be noted that Japan is one of the world's most vulnerable countries, much more vulnerable than it was during the Second World War. For that reason Japan risks either being too heavily destroyed to rebuild, or capitulating before sufficient damage has been done for the war to work as an economic stimulus afterward.

From this we can now draw one simple conclusion. If war can lead both to destruction and to construction, the same probably applies to peace. As we well know, from conditions of absence of violence of the direct kind, both the most despotic and the most democratic, can emerge both the poorest and the richest types of societies. So there is no simple relationship. But does the same apply to steps toward peace, to the *process* leading from war to peace? Even if the *goal* of peace in the conventional sense can be combined with all kinds of levels of economic growth, is there a process from here to there?

In other words, what is the status of the thesis, so long cherished by the peace movement, that disarmament is a road both to peace and to development? Melting swords into plowshares, as it is expressed in the Bible. The argument is well known and has much appeal. Reducing armament costs means reducing the capacity to wage war; investing the savings wisely could bring about development. Two birds killed with one stone—a genius operation that only fools could fail to carry out! The idea is supported by reasoning in terms of opportunity costs: 900–1,000 billion dollars spent annually on armaments are converted to basic needs units—to food, clothing, shelter, medical services, and schooling units. Only one missile or bomber plane can be shown to represent opportunity costs that make a difference for small countries in such units. Ruth Sivard's important series, *World Military and Social Expenditures,*[4] gives excellent information in this perspective. Of course, the two superpowers, with 11% of the world population, spend more than half of the world's military budget and 80% of the military research budget. They—particularly the United States with 43% of the U.S. army stationed abroad[5]—occupy military bases throughout the world, account for 53% of arms efforts, and control 97% of all nuclear weapons.

Since "peace and development" are the two major concerns of humankind, and also of the United Nations, the idea of choking off funds for the military, and at the same time getting development really going, sounds particularly brilliant to U.N. ears. However, there are three rather major difficulties.

First, it is not at all obvious that less money to the military leads to peace or even to disarmament. The military machine functions like any other system of production: on the basis of capital, labor, raw materials, and research. Reduce the capital, take the money away, make the military system less capital-intensive, and the system will immediately go in for more research-intensive approaches producing a "bigger bang for the buck" and "more rubble for the ruble." It could also go back to more labor-intensive methods of producing destruction, mobilizing the whole population one way or the other. But then, even if this should lead to a real reduction in military destructiveness—and money taken away from military research probably would—it is not at all safe to assume that it would lead to peace. Disarmament may not even be a road to peace at all. It could well be that "transarmament," toward defensive forms of defense, with emphasis on short distance and smart rockets, paramilitary forces, and nonmilitary resistance (civil disobedience, nonviolence) is what is needed, as there will always be a problem of security. And that may still be costly. Security needs do not disappear together with military budgets. The world is not that simple.

Second, it is not at all obvious that more money leads to development. Iran had no scarcity of money during the period of the late shah—yet, was there development? Development, it seems, is more a question of autonomy, of being sufficiently free to really satisfy the basic needs of the people and promote ecological balance. It is a question of building strong people rather than merely trying to build strong elites and strong countries—with rich upper classes, strong military establishments, and high but undistributed GNP. The experience seems to be that the more money is available the more will it be used for capital-intensive approaches that are very good for building strong elites and strong countries. But to build strong people— healthy, well fed, well educated, autonomous, cooperative—hard work is needed. A little money helps. Very much money may just plaster over the structural problems for a time, until the whole structure explodes, as we saw in the case of Iran and probably shall see in most *nouveaux riches* countries in the years to come.

Third, the relation between peace and development is supposed to be defined and worked out at the international level, between countries. Most spending for the military is found in the rich countries, and most development deficits in the poor countries. Are the rich countries really supposed to give those giant sums to poor countries when the rich themselves are in tremendous difficulties economically? Is it not more reasonable to assume that if they should reduce their military budgets, then they would put that money to use inside

their own countries, eliminating their own development deficits? In
the case of the United States, for instance, should it not be used to
stop the increasing slummification of the cities, giving jobs to poor
people for that purpose? And in Soviet Russia to finance the giant
perestroika?

In other words, if conversion is to be carried out, it is much more
likely to be conversion within rather than between countries. This
might also be the better solution, given that countries are not known
to give away money easily without strings attached. Are we really so
naive as to assume that if the superpowers should give away much of
their military funds for development in the poor parts of the world,
they would not then be sitting on top of that money, seeing to it that
it is applied the way they want, according to their ideas of what con-
stitutes development, not to mention their ideas of security needs?
Will the basic human needs approach and ecological balance be on
top of their minds?

In short, I find the idea too simplistic. That does not mean there is
no linkage between disarmament and development. There certainly
is, but the linkage is probably within rather than between countries.
A country that today would engage in transarmament, putting its
defense budget into conventional, defensive weapons, and at the
same time would try to make itself less vulnerable through more self-
reliance, nationally and locally, would make a tremendous contribution to peace and to its own development.

If the economic approach does not seem so promising, how about a
more structural approach to the linkage between peace and development? Switching to this perspective, the whole relationship suddenly
becomes more simple, and we can easily see very concrete policies
hinted at above that would promote both peace and development.

- *At the international level:* establishing equitable, really equitable,
  cooperation between countries, which tends to be a peace-building
  measure. The countries create a symbiotic relationship and at the
  same time promote development in both countries·through exchange of ideas, goods, services, and people, with neither country
  dominating the other. The problem is the difficulty in doing this
  between big and small countries, or between rich and poor countries—indicating that cooperation, to be peace- and development-
  building, perhaps should be mainly between equals. This seems,
  incidentally, now to be the emerging pattern: superpower-super-

power, north-north, south-south relations are being strengthened all over the place. But there is still much work to be done.

- *At the national level:* making the country more self-*sufficient* in such essentials as food, health, and energy inputs, and in general self-reliant so that the country is (1) less tempted to go to war against others to get economic essentials (such as oil) and (2) less tempting for others as a target of food/health/energy weapons, thereby increasing world tension. At the same time this may promote development by laying a basis for self-*reliance,* which is a combination of self-sufficiency in essentials and equitable relations with other countries for less essential goods and services.

- *At the local level:* making the local level more self-reliant and more autonomous, more powerful—thereby both strengthening the local level and weakening the central level so that the center (the bureaucrats, the corporations, the intelligentsia, the military, the police, and sometimes the party) is less able to exploit the people and to accumulate enough surplus to wage aggressive wars.

The concept that best summarizes this approach is probably the concept used a number of times above already: self-reliance,[6] but at all three levels, local, national, and regional (e.g., Third World). Unfortunately, this is far from the dominant development practice today. Consequently, I do not think we are building much peace either.

To summarize: The relation between peace and development is complex because the processes relating to them are themselves so complicated in the present world. "Peace" is good and "development" is good. But what if the machinery needed for war, militarization, is also the machinery needed for development: a strong centralized leadership; vertical, hierarchical organizations; planning at the top and blind obedience at the bottom, combined with bread and circuses? I have suggested structural change, smaller units tied together in equitable exchange relations, possibly in federal structures. I have tried to indicate that such structures may be more successful in achieving both true development and more peaceful relations.

But what if war nevertheless comes? Can such structures also offer a country's inhabitants sufficient security through defense? The answer

is probably yes, but by changing the military rather than by abolishing it. As mentioned, there are concepts of defense much more compatible with decentralized social structures. One is violent: small, decentralized military, including paramilitary (guerrilla) units. The other is nonviolent: the whole repertoire of ideas for nonmilitary defense. To go in for them is to go in for *trans*armament rather than a *dis*armament that would merely make people defenseless. In fact, these are the ways in which people tend to organize themselves against external and internal repression; so there are lots of experiences to draw upon. But it is not the general approach pursued by the states in the contemporary world, with the quest for central control leading to a quest for centralized responses to any functional or structural problem society may encounter, because the power is in the center.

In conclusion: The key to a policy that may, at least in the longer run, lead to gains both in terms of peace and in terms of development lies in some structural change predictably resisted by those who consider the costs too high. The narrow definitions in terms of "development = economic growth" and "peace = absence of war" stimulate large-scale bureaucratic/corporate exploitation and militarization machines, preferred by many at the top of the structure. To take money from one and give to the other will not change the logic of the structure they have in common in any significant, peace-productive way. More focus on the deeper levels of our existence—*nature space* with ecological balance; *human space* with basic human needs; *social space* with self-reliance—seems so much more promising for both peace and development in *world space*.

CHAPTER 2

The Cold War, Peace, and Development: A Comparison of the Atlantic and Pacific Theaters

A PLEA FOR GLOBALISM AND WHOLISM

Most Europeans, East and West, but probably not most North Americans, seem to be of the opinion that the Cold War is something found only in the Atlantic area, between the United States and Western Europe on the one hand, and the Soviet Union and Eastern Europe on the other, with some neutral countries interspersed. Of course, this is a Eurocentric vision. Much of the Cold War, even considerably more than in the Atlantic area, is found in the Pacific area, between the United States and its allies on the one hand and the Soviet Union and its former and present allies on the other, with some neutral countries interspersed. It is in this part of the world, far away from Europeans, that two major wars after the Second World War have been fought: the Korean War, 1950–53, and the two Indochina wars, 1945–75. This is the region where the Cold War became hot. In the complex tangle of reasons why, perhaps, one stands out: the temperature of the war was mainly a problem for "Asiatics," although many U.S. soldiers also lost their lives (one major reason why the United States cannot be accused of Eurocentrism or Atlantocentrism). Nor the Soviet Union, for that matter.[1]

In a similar vein, very many people tend to look at "peace" and "development" as two separate issues, the former being "east-west" and the latter "north-south." Like the separation between the Atlantic and the Pacific, which is not only conceptual but also geographic, this distinction is not only geographic but also conceptual and serves some purpose by directing our attention to the danger of a major war and the ever-present misery and its reproduction. And yet the conceptual separation has been driven too far. Interconnections between peace and development may be lost. And similarly for the Atlantic/ Pacific distinction; not only interrelations, but also obvious similarities and dissimilarities between what will now be referred to as the two theaters of the Cold War may easily be lost sight of. Hence, this exercise in a more global and wholistic approach, an attempt to see the Atlantic and Pacific theaters from a common vantage point, exploring how peace and development go hand-in-hand in a structure that essentially was the product of the Second World War.

A GENERAL THEORY OF THE COLD WAR

Let us start by simply asking a question: What does it take to make a Cold War, with its tremendous domain and scope, covering so much of the world, even with the possible extinction of major parts of the world as a consequence? How did we ever get into that kind of structure/process, evolving every day, spreading in domain and deepening in scope, and usually in a way which seems to make a mockery of both peace and development (although there are also some reversals to this negative process)?

Let us try to reason at the general level, yet keeping elementary history of post-Second World War relations present in our minds. What do we see, forty years in retrospect? Of course, back in spring and summer 1945, from May till August, we see the victors and the defeated, in principle the Allies and the Axis powers. However, among the Axis powers, Italy, with a characteristic sense of the dialectics of history, managed to rid itself of what seemed to be an indelible stamp as Axis power, joined the victors, and emerged almost an ally. And on the other side, although there were many victors, there was no doubt in anybody's mind that the United States of America and the Union of Soviet Socialist Republics were in a class all by themselves—the former having contributed materially in an absolutely major sense, the latter having lost 20 million Soviet lives, and with 10 million of the 13.6 million German soldiers (95% of whom were on the eastern front before the Normandy invasion of June 1944) who were killed during the war fallen on Soviet soil. One paid for the victory, including payment in human sacrifice; the other paid with human sacrifice and material destruction on a scale previously almost unheard of.[2]

Of course, there were also Great Britain who had managed to stave off the enemy, and France and China who had not managed to do so. They had been partly, even wholly, occupied by the Germans and the Japanese, respectively, but managed to put up a resistance creditable enough that they could be present among the Potsdam powers, although in the case of China only by cable.[3]

When I now count only the two powers, subsequently to be termed as superpowers, as *the* victors, it is essentially for four reasons.

First, each entered the war against the Axis powers with a basic traumatic experience: Operation Barbarossa, 22 June 1941, for the Soviet Union; Pearl Harbor, 7 December 1941, for the United States —surprise attacks that shaped their image of world events in general and military doctrine in particular, providing them with a strong NEVERMORE ideology.

Second, both superpowers came out of the war with a very high level of self-righteousness. Both regarded their own contributions to the defeat of the Axis as not only necessary, but to a large extent as sufficient. The abysmal moral quality of the enemy made the victors look perfect. The self-righteousness derived not only from the magnitude of the effort to defeat him, but also from the depravity of the defeated party. The feeling of having done away with vermin, with pests, was strong—and to a large extent justified.

Third, both powers were new on the world scene, essentially creations of the First World War. Both of them were strongly ideological in their world outlooks, liberal/conservative/capitalist versus marxist/socialist. In short, both of them had programs. Both of them knew what would be good not only for themselves but for the whole world.

And fourth, whereas the preceding three points make them look similar, this last point sets them far apart: Both knew perfectly well that their ideologies were incompatible, that their models for socio-economic (re-)construction were also incompatible, and that their interests to a large extent might also be incompatible—for instance, the U.S. interest in market penetration and the Soviet interest in a geopolitical buffer zone around Soviet territory. But incompatibility of values *or* interests already spells conflict; incompatibility of values *and* interests may even spell deep conflict. And they knew equally well that they had been at loggerheads before the war, that they had been brought together in an uneasy alliance, both of them suspecting that the other would make separate peace with Nazi Germany and that a friendship based on little more than "the enemy of my enemy is my friend" factor might be of short duration. A self-fulfilling prophecy.

What did the defeated countries look like? They left the war deeply humiliated, certainly not self-righteously. However, there is a difference between Germany and Japan in this regard. In both countries almost the whole population was mobilized and continued fighting to the very end. Open opposition was small, insignificant. And yet the Nazi leaders were more different from the ordinary German than were the Japanese leaders from the Japanese people. One can to some extent draw a line around the Nazi leaders, count them, arraign them into court, and even punish them. A similar exercise for the Japanese would almost have to be futile, given the collectivist nature of the country and the amount of consensus between elite and people.[4]

Of course both countries also left the war deeply wounded. The defeat was a major traumatic experience, the sequel of which we do not as yet know. The destruction of Berlin, the dismemberment of Germany, and the plunder after the war may be seen as revenge for Operation Barbarossa; the nuclear genocide committed against the populations of Hiroshima and Nagasaki also as revenge for Pearl Harbor. How, or whether, the revenge will be revenged we do not know today.

Whatever damage the Nazi powers had inflicted on the Allies on the Western side was amply revenged in saturation/carpet bombing, even to excess. But the wounds inflicted on the Soviet Union were of such depth and magnitude that no commensurate revenge could be found, given the short duration of the fight on German soil. Except, and this is important: the dismemberment of the German Reich in the east into three parts, some of it absorbed into the Soviet Union, some of it into Poland, and some of it constituting what today is known as the DDR, the German Democratic Republic. And then there is BRD, the Federal Republic of Germany, and the situation of West Berlin, and of East Berlin—a Reich divided, indeed.

Did the defeated countries emerge with a program? Of course they did: after such a total war and such a total defeat, they emerged with the programs of their victors. What else could they do? They could not continue, at least not overtly, with their old programs. Their "crimes against humanity" had been of such magnitude that the past had to be disavowed, at least for some time. The war, having been at least partly ideological, carried in its wake an ideological peace where the defeated countries had to confess their sins, reject their pasts, including their inhuman ideologies, atone, and declare themselves on line with the victors. The victors wanted not only unconditional surrender but also total defeat: a prostrate, defeated country, not only willing, but asking, to receive the Word, the imprint of the victor.

In so doing conflict was courted. The conflict between the super-powers with their super-ideologies was transmitted to the defeated countries who then learned to express their world views, second in line only to the superpowers. Some kind of peace with the victor was gained at the expense of ever-deepening conflict with the other victor and "his" defeated country. The relationship was, and is, a tight one: the major characteristics of the situation of the victors would necessarily have to be reflected in the situation of the defeated countries; all three of them (West and East Germany, and Japan—not counting Italy).

However, much more is needed for a group of victorious and defeated countries to produce that solid structure/process known as the Cold War today. The last two elements mentioned, the missionary calling of the program, and the emerging conflict, would have to be whipped into shape as an ideology. That ideology took both positive and negative forms. The positive aspect was a model of development: liberal/capitalist versus marxist/socialist, the models of the superpowers. The defeated countries had a vested interest in good relations with the victors, and the victors were ever present as occupation armies, busily working to implement their programs at any point, implanting their genetic code wherever they could in suitable carrying mechanisms: multiparty versus single-party systems; market economies versus centrally planned economies. The defeated countries started increasingly to come out like clones, leaning over backward to perform their roles; the distance between cloning and clowning being a short one, not only phonetically.

But the ideology had also a negative component, with one side being anti-communist in general and anti-Soviet Union and/or anti-Moscow, in particular, and the other side being anti-imperialist and anti-United States or perhaps rather anti-Washington, in particular. Pre-war incidents and attitudes were invoked, a short term war alliance gradually suppressed or even successfully forgotten, new post-war incidents and attitudes being sedimented on top of old ideological baggage. At this point it should not be forgotten that the 1917 revolution was a major trauma for the West, with the brutal killing of

Tsar Nicolai II in Yekaterinburg (Sverdlovsk) as the major event, just as the interventionist wars of 1918–22 constituted a major trauma for the new Soviet Union. Like the United States one and a half centuries earlier, the Soviet Union was built on a considerable basis of elite and popular idealism, and had also suffered interventionist wars.

And yet, ideology alone would never have been sufficient. Something more was needed, and a particularly nasty component was brought into the recipe for the Cold War. I am thinking of the divided nations, not only of the idea of drawing a line across somebody else's territory, but of enrolling the two parts in the two blocs. People in the two parts of divided countries had to take opposite sides, and the conflict was fanned by the emotional—to the point of fratricidal—energies associated with internal as opposed to ordinary external wars. Two such countries became particularly important: divided Germany with divided Berlin in its midst, and divided Korea. Of course these were the places where the Cold War became extremely tense (Berlin 1948/49) and even very hot (Korea 1950–53) because of built-in conflict production. And then there was a third, Vietnam (1945–75); the incredible country that defeated Japan, France, the United States, and—to some extent—even China, in the course of one generation.[5] And it is the only one of the three that succeeded in getting united.

These were the three decisive processes that served to produce one more step: lining up like-minded and like-interested countries in alliances. Obviously, for a country to enter into alliance with a superpower it is not necessary to hate the other superpower. It is not even necessary to be anti-communist or anti-imperialist. All that is needed is to assume that "the enemy of my friend is my enemy," and for some reason to accept a superpower as friend. The latter may be done on the basis of ideological similarity or interest, literally speaking, in the program presented for development. Where peace/war issues end and development/maldevelopment issues begin in this extremely complex web of values and interests is impossible to state in general terms; nor is it very important. A good example is the Spanish elite being taught that Spain is threatened by Soviet invasion, an implausible idea; Spain being very far from a communist take-over. But the use of NATO membership for the modernization of Spain and "entry into Europe" is highly plausible.[6]

The process may also run counter to what was just said: driven by intense anti-imperialism or anti-communism, the conclusion can be that "the enemy of my enemy must be my friend," and an alliance with a superpower is then the next step. The cognitive triangle involved is actually the same, the logic is the same, the conclusion is the same—only the premises are organized a little differently. It is enough that the elites think in the way just mentioned; they will probably be in command of foreign policy anyhow. They may be of the same opinion. The people may be marginalized, alienated, apathetic, leaving the whole foreign policy game to the *classe politique*. But they may also be dead against, having just the opposite views. In that case, people will draw the conclusion that the other superpower, being the enemy of the superpower selected by their own hated elite, cannot possibly be bad: "the enemy of the friend of my enemy is my friend."[7] As can be noted, the chains are now becoming somewhat long and unwieldy. They might easily break if one of the links in the chain is exposed as weak, even blatantly wrong. And that is exactly what Cold War propaganda from both sides tries to show or deny.

Let us now add one very important element in the total recipe: to enroll the defeated country as the most faithful ally. It is not an unproblematic policy. On the one hand, the defeated country is easily blackmailed into posturing as the best pupil in the class, and this may set a model for others to follow. But it may also happen, on the other hand, that others do not like to follow a model set by the former enemy. On the contrary, they may have the suspicion that some kind of collusion between the victorious superpower and the formerly hated, defeated country is going on, that they have become too cozy and that this is all directed against the rest of the alliance. Hence, the superpower has to exercise some political talent in the effort to make use of the defeated country as most faithful ally. The United States has probably been more fortunate with the Federal Republic of Germany than with Japan in this regard, partly for the reason mentioned above that Japan changed less, or less in depth, as a result of defeat, and partly because of less sensitivity to East Asian than to European affairs and relations, the latter being more similar to those of the United States.

However, no system can remain perfect. If there is a most faithful ally there is also the most unfaithful, the ally that opts out of the system. Theoretically, he has two possibilities: to join the other alliance, or to become nonaligned/neutral. Whatever he does, he may remain

Figure 1. A Cold War System

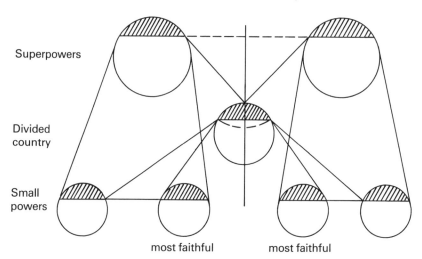

in that position or change again, in which case he will probably be classified as a maverick, not merely as unfaithful. There is also another possibility, "the unfaithful of all camps, unite," constituting a new alliance; but that seems to be a more theoretical outcome.

Let us now construct a figure from these possible relationships (Fig. 1). Circles represent countries, superpowers on top, a divided one in the middle, and other allies at the bottom; each country is shown divided into elites and people, center and periphery. The two broken lines stand for the basic negative relations, the two central unbroken lines for the basic positive relations in the game; the other lines are built around this nucleus.

The nucleus of the Cold War consists of superpowers, divided countries, and most faithful countries, based on very solid sentiments. Needless to say, the figure becomes much more complicated if the people do not agree with the elite; in other words, if there are not only dissidents, but dissident movements, a dissident people, even to the point where the elite might have preferred "to elect a new people" (East Berlin and DDR 1953—Bertolt Brecht). The total construction is based on elite allegiance rather than on country allegiance, assuming the elites are sufficiently in control to guarantee the superpowers military access; that is, bases, nuclear task forces, command of the military forces in case of war (and for maneuvers, etc., in peacetime).

There seem to be two different superpower strategies. The first would be to build on popular elites really supported by their population, provided the country as a whole is not both anti-Washington and anti-Moscow. The second strategy would be to build on unpopular elites, guaranteeing them against popular wrath, even to the point of coming to their rescue in case of revolts/revolutions, in return for complete loyalty according to the usual conflict polarization scheme. In Europe, the United States has been using strategy No. 1 and the Soviet Union strategy No. 2, *grosso modo;* this is perhaps not so strange since the United States liberated Nazi-occupied countries in Western Europe, while the Soviet Union defeated Axis regimes in Eastern Europe (with the exception of Poland, of course) and installed their own.

For the Soviet Union, both strategies are problematic. In countries where communism, or at least the regime, was popular, the whole population turned against the Soviet Union (Yugoslavia, Albania, China). In countries where communism was unpopular the people turned against both elites and the Soviet Union, with the latter coming to the rescue of the former in bloody interventions (Hungary, 1956; Czechoslovakia, 1968; Afghanistan, 1979—and, in a more indirect way, Poland, 1981).

So much for the general theory of the Cold War. Let us now turn to the two manifestations, the two theaters.

THE ATLANTIC AND PACIFIC THEATERS COMPARED

In Table 1 the reader will find a systematic comparison between the Atlantic and Pacific theaters in the Cold War. Very often this is referred to as the East-West conflict, with the understanding that "East" is the Soviet Union and the Warsaw Treaty Organization (WTO) and "West" is the United States and NATO. This, however, is Eurocentric/Atlantocentric: in the Pacific/East Asian theater the United States is to the east and the Soviet Union to the west. Hence, it is better to use ideological terms and refer to the conflict as a conflict between capitalism and socialism, in other words (in the view of the present author), as a conflict between two systems rather than between two parts of global geography.

Table 1. The Cold War: The Atlantic and Pacific Theaters Compared

Dimensions	ATLANTIC		PACIFIC	
	Capitalist (West)	Socialist (East)	Capitalist (East)	Socialist (West)
1. Victorious countries	US (2) (GB, F)	SU (1)	US (1) (China)	SU (2)
2. Defeated countries	West Germany (I)	East Germany (H, R, BG; ČS, YU)	Japan	
3. Ideology	Liberalism / Conservatism Anti - communism Development	Marxism Anti - imperialism Development	Liberalism / Conservatism Anti - communism Development	Marxism Anti - imperialism Development
4. Divided countries	West Germany (Austria)	East Germany + Polish territory + Soviet territory (A, SF, Pl, ČS, H, R)	South Korea Japan (Okinawa) Taiwan (Hong Kong, Macao) South Vietnam	North Korea Four Islands China North Vietnam
5. Alliance systems	NATO	WTO	US - Japan US - South Korea US - Taiwan US - South Vietnam	SU - Mongolia SU - North Korea SU - China SU - North Vietnam
6. Most faithful country = defeated country	BRD (I)	DDR (BG)	Japan	
7. Unfaithful country (protest countries)	France (GR? NL? B? DK?)	Rumania Yugoslavia, Albania, (Pl, H, ČS)	(New Zealand in ANZUS)	China
8. Independent country	France	Yugoslavia (Albania)		China (North Korea?)

Let us then look at the eight lines in the table. They are placed in the same order as in the presentation of the general theory of the Cold War in the preceding section, with examples.

The victors are very clear, but they have been equipped with some numerals in the table to indicate which was the major and which the second victor in the two theaters. Under the United States has been added Great Britain and France for the Atlantic theater, and China (both Nationalist and Communist, who were fighting together against Japan) for the Pacific theater. But they do not add anything to the analysis since a basic point here is that the Cold War conflict is primarily a superpower conflict. Only the superpowers had super-ideologies, programs designed to fit the whole world. Only they were the potential creators of world-systems and holders of super-weapons, weapons so strong that their use can be justified only against super-enemies. In addition, they saw themselves as the not only necessary but sufficient causes for the defeat of the Nazi powers. Other countries may satisfy some of these conditions but not all of them; that is the privilege of the United States and the Soviet Union.

Then, in the second line, are the defeated countries, the Axis countries, with some lesser members underneath. It may be noted that, whereas the United States had powerful allies, they actually defeated only West Germany and to some extent Italy. The Soviet Union was fighting alone, but defeated not only East Germany, but also the other Axis countries—Hungary, Rumania, Bulgaria, parts of Czechoslovakia, and Yugoslavia. In the Pacific theater, however, no country can really be said to have capitulated to the Soviet Union, which entered the war only one week before it was over, in agreement with Yalta-Potsdam (but certainly not with the Soviet Union–Japan pact). The job was done by the United States (and China).[8]

The ideology is clear, written into the headings of the table. It varies in meaning all the time, but both in terms of allies and in terms of interests of elites and people, the differences are very real. Whether the dominant economic system is market or central planning does make a difference.

Then, we turn to the divided countries. They are more numerous than people usually realize. On the European side there is of course Germany, divided into four parts, as mentioned, although the focus is on the Federal Republic of Germany and the German Democratic Republic. However, Austria, Finland, Poland, Czechoslovakia, Hungary, and Rumania were also divided as a result of the war. Sentiments in that connection continue riding high, meaning that there are emotions that can be played upon in various ways.

In the Pacific theater one usually thinks of Korea as the divided country; often, unfairly, it is compared with Germany. Korea was treated by the victors as a part of Japan and the Japanese war effort, and the Korean—to a large extent, heroic—resistance fight was not recognized as such. Korea was divided, probably because giving the Soviet Union control over a part of Korea was found to be preferable to giving what the Soviet Union might have liked: Hokkaido. The United States wanted Japan for herself, but the Soviet Union was given the four famous Japanese South Kuril islands (one of them is a small archipelago). And the United States got Okinawa. Thus Japan was also a divided country as a result of the war, and so was, later on, China with the People's Republic on the one hand and the Republic of China (Taiwan) on the other, leaving out Hong Kong and Macao. And in addition to this, as mentioned above, was Vietnam, also divided in the aftermath of the war, and in a major way.

When we now turn to the alliances, their names and shapes are very well known in the Atlantic theater because of NATO and WTO. In the Pacific theater they are less clear cut, consisting of a number of bilateral, perhaps to some extent trilateral, constructions.[9] The United States has her security treaties with Japan (AMPO), South Korea, and Taiwan (and at some time with Vietnam). The Soviet Union has her arrangements with Mongolia, North Korea, and Vietnam (and at some time with the People's Republic of China). Farther south the United States has various arrangements with the ASEAN countries (bases—SEATO) and ANZUS; the Soviet Union nothing.

There is no doubt as to who are the most faithful allies; by this logic these are the defeated countries, BRD and DDR in the Atlantic theater, and Japan in the Pacific theater—again leaving the Soviet Union out in the cold with no faithful ally. I have added Italy in parentheses for the Western superpower and Bulgaria in parentheses for the Eastern one. Both of them were Axis countries; both of them have repented and joined the fold. But they were not the major Axis countries. Italy was an ally in the First World War, and Bulgaria feels close to Russia for cultural and historical (the war against Turkey) reasons.

Then the unfaithful allies. There is no doubt which are the major ones: France, Yugoslavia, China. But we have also added some lesser ones in parentheses, the most recent entry into this field being New

Zealand with the refusal (February 1985) to accept U.S. warships that may (but also may not) have nuclear devices.

And, at the bottom, the independent actors have been added. There are not many of them, at least for the time being, and only one maverick country: Albania (there is also the possibility that North Korea may play a similar role in East Asia). One may of course discuss how independent the independent actors are, discipline being the rule. Maverick countries are there to be rejected by both sides, like *Die Grünen* in Germany rejected by blue and red alike as a "maverick party" even when it is not.

These are the major points, using the general recipe for a Cold War as developed in the preceding section. In order to gain more depth in this presentation, let us now point out some major differences between the Atlantic and Pacific theaters, the similarities being only too clearly evident from the table. And let us take as point of departure the Atlantic situation and show how the Pacific situation differs, proceeding line by line.

First, although the Second World War determines the logic of the scheme, there was no balance between the two superpowers as they emerged from the war. The United States was so much more important. That changed four years after the war, on 1 October 1949, with the victory of the communist revolution in China and the Soviet-China treaty based on the idea of "eternal friendship." And it changed again, equally dramatically, about ten years later when the rift between the two communist powers—the largest country in the world and the most populous country in the world—became increasingly apparent, exploding in open hostility another ten years later, in 1969 (the Ussuri River incident). In other words, the logic of the power balance is also determined by the internal dynamism of the blocs and the "development" of the countries, not only by the massive belligerent interaction known as the Second World War.[10]

Second, very much related to this, the Soviet Union had nobody capitulating to them in the Pacific theater, North Korea being an artifact. This is important, influencing the way the Soviet Union was treating China. Maybe China was regarded as "theirs," in the same way that the United States regarded Japan? To the Soviet Union the Nationalist government had been an enemy; during the war its forces were fighting on the same side against the Axis; and then, four years after the war, that government was defeated, the enmity being continued from Taiwan. So maybe there was an ambiguity in the Soviet attitude to China: on the one hand, the Communist party had come into power; on the other hand, China as a country had been defeated. Such attitudes may take the form of self-fulfilling prophecies turning friends into enemies, thereby confirming to the Soviet Union that they were right in seeing China as a defeated enemy. However, regardless of how that might have been, the slot is empty as far as the Second World War is concerned. The Pacific theater capitulation was to the United States, not to the Soviet Union.

Third, the ideology. There is a difference. In the Pacific theater the ideology is much more concerned with internal enemies. The internal contradictions, usually related to class in one way or another, are much stronger, much more pronounced, more similar to South America, Africa, the rest of Asia. A regime is threatened by its internal opposition. The (oligarchic) elites turn against the opposition, well knowing that they can get support from a superpower by casting the opposition in the role of subversive forces acting for the other superpower. Plots and spies and agents turn up everywhere. The picture is certainly not unknown in the Atlantic theater, but there is an asymmetry in quantity if not in quality.[11]

Fourth, the divided countries. There are two major differences: in the Atlantic theater, the defeated country was the divided country; in the Pacific theater, a colony of Japan was forced into that role. The immediate assumption would be that this creates even more emotional energy in the Korean case, derived from the feeling of being totally unjustly treated by history. The Germans have, after all, a sense that horrendous crimes were committed and that division was the punishment, too light or too heavy depending on how the matter is evaluated, but perhaps useful for prevention and atonement. The Koreans have no such sense at all, nor do they see any reason why *they* should atone.

And this is where the Cold War became hot, already in 1950. Even thirty-five years after the armistice in 1953 nothing basic has changed. The Koreans may rightly draw the conclusion that their obligation is to stay divided to provide Cold War conflict energy and not rock the boat; that the present abnormal situation is considered the normal situation by outsiders and that nobody cares as much for Germany, possibly for racist reasons. Much of the same attitude was expressed in the situation in Vietnam, but an extremely bloody war took place and the result was unification. Japan also got Okinawa back, China will ultimately get Hong Kong and Macao. But when or whether Japan will get the four islands to the north back again, and Taiwan will join China, are still for the future to see; as is also the case for the two Koreas. My guess, an intuition, might be that by the year 2000 they will all be united.[12]

Something is relatively clear: there has been more dynamism in connection with the divided countries in East Asia, and it will probably continue that way, than with the divided countries in Europe. The big exception is, of course, Austria in 1955—exchanging unification for neutrality. If that formula were to be applied to all the divided countries in East Asia, it is easily seen that the United States would lose more than would the Soviet Union. It would lose Japan, South Korea, and Taiwan; the Soviet Union only North Korea— China already having been lost and Vietnam already having been gained (although both could be adjusted, retroactively). As to the other divided countries in Europe: for the countries bordering on the Soviet Union, it looks as if the borders are permanent (the Final Act of Helsinki), but some formula for the two Germanys might still be found in exchange for neutrality, at least nuclear neutrality. The Soviet Union would then probably have to throw more countries into the bargain (Rapacki Plan) to obtain "balance," at least in Europe.

Fifth, when one looks at the alliance systems, there is a remarkable difference: multilateralism in the Atlantic theater, bilateralism in the Pacific theater. There may be many reasons for the latter. No doubt one reason is that the countries related to the United States are not contiguous, and the countries related to the Soviet Union were contiguous only as long as China was included. But all three of them had problematic relations to China: the allies of the United States were separated only by ocean, the allies of the Soviet Union by China. Second, there is less of a cultural/historical bond; the relationships are recent and usually negative. Third, and this may be the most important factor, the countries are less streamlined ideologically, possibly because Asians, and particularly Asians influenced by Chinese culture, may have a more ambiguous, more dialectical approach to conflict. China had every reason to be anti-imperialist when one hundred years of history, from the Opium Wars of the 1840s until the fight against the Nationalist forces, supported by Western powers, came to an end in 1949.

And yet, where is China today? More anti-communist in the sense of anti-Moscow, than anti-imperialist in the sense of anti-Washington, for sure. But if such a major switch has happened once, it can happen twice; the ambiguity may be resolved in another direction, once more.[13] It must be very difficult for a superpower to preside over such countries. Perhaps it would be better to deal with them one at a time, in a system of bilateralism, than in a multilateral treaty organization where their ambiguities might one day be aligned against the superpowers!

It is not difficult to imagine how messy this must look, particularly in the eyes of Washington—less so in the eyes of Moscow, itself not alien to more Oriental perspectives in politics. Washington must have been itching for some kind of PATO (Pacific Area Treaty Organization) paralleling NATO, with headquarters some place in the eastern part of East Asia (Singapore?) paralleling Brussels, with Hawaii playing a role similar to that of the Canaries and Azores, maybe even with a joint NATO/PATO secretariat in Washington. I would doubt that Moscow is itching for the same thing, being more geared to bilateralism in general.[14]

Sixth, in the Pacific the Soviet Union has no most faithful country generated by the Second World War for the reason that there is no defeated country that capitulated to the Soviet Union. Mongolia is of earlier vintage, created under quite different conditions after the First World War.[15] In Europe the two superpowers have their Germanys and in addition one Axis power each, as somebody to be counted upon: Italy on the one hand, Bulgaria on the other. The United States has Japan who plays her role with diligence, but possibly also with a subtlety that one day may come as a surprise for the United States (*vide* the remark about trauma from the nuclear onslaught, above).

Seventh, there is also a remarkable difference when it comes to unfaithful countries. In East Asia not only does the Soviet Union have no "most faithful country"; it certainly has also had an "unfaithful country": China, leaving the bilateral relationship. The United States suffered no similar ignominy in the Pacific theater. It is only most recently that a protest country has appeared: New Zealand, a small one, but nonetheless threatening to wreck the ANZUS alliance. In Europe the Soviet Union has also suffered more losses than the other superpower. Yugoslavia left in 1948, Albania in 1961, and around that time Rumania became considerably less integrated in the military aspect of the Warsaw Treaty Organization, in a position not much different from that of France after 1965–66. Both superpowers have their share of protest countries, but the differences are tremendous. Hungary was even taken out of WTO in 1956 for a very short period. Sentiments in Poland and Czechoslovakia have definitely been in the same direction, WTO having been one element in the revolts and interventions (counting the Soviet intervention in Poland as structural rather than direct).[16] The protests and hesitations against nuclear armament by the governments of Greece, Netherlands, Belgium, and Denmark have not led to such dramatic reactions. The pressure has been brought to bear on New Zealand in the ANZUS system—the trilateral organization of the United States with New Zealand and Australia—no doubt as a warning to other protest countries, possibly also because New Zealand is more isolated in its setting than are the European protest countries in theirs[17] and hence more easily dealt with precisely because the setting is more bilateral.

Eighth, the Soviet camp has produced two clearly independent actors: Yugoslavia and China. The U.S. camp produced one for a short period: France under De Gaulle, today a somewhat irregular member of the system. The Soviet camp may be said to have produced two maverick countries that do not join the international system, keeping aside, being isolated and for that reason "unpredictable": Albania and North Korea. On the other hand, it is also clear that not only have there been better reasons, it has also been easier, in the sense of more frequent incidents, to leave the Soviet camp than the U.S. camp. Yugoslavia, Albania, China, and then partly Rumania, all give testimony to the falsity of the thesis that once a country has come into the socialist camp the process is irreversible. Looking at the evidence, the opposite hypothesis might have more plausibility, that countries are free to join the Western alliance but not free to leave.[18] Countries were *not* free to join the Eastern alliance, they were enrolled—no doubt creating tensions which make it more likely that they will leave. To leave the U.S. camp is more of a protest, hence more of a blow to the country.

This, of course, does not mean that it was easy for anybody to leave. The exit tickets for France and China were rather similar: an independent nuclear force.[19] As big powers they wanted big weapons. They also wanted to make it absolutely clear that they could hold their own against their former superpower, not only against the superpower on the other side. For lesser powers the exit tickets may be less dramatic. Yugoslavia has paid with a high level of conventional military readiness; Albania in addition with isolation, feeling that neither a former enemy (the capitalist powers) nor the new enemy (the socialist powers), nor the newest enemy (China), and indeed not the age-old enemy (Yugoslavia) merits their active coexistence. And Austria paid her price, neutrality. Which price Rumania is paying is unclear, but it may have something to do with the economically catastrophic condition of that country.[20]

For all of these non-nuclear protest countries, however, the price may be a blessing in disguise: a higher level of security by being non-nuclear, having little in terms of offensive arms, and a high level of defensive readiness, at the same time as they are decoupled from the superpower. Other countries might like to do the same. Hungary in 1956 was no doubt inspired by the old partner in the Austro-Hungarian double monarchy the year before; all the other protest countries, East and West, may have or may develop similar visions. It is not easy to be a superpower, presiding over large portions of humankind according to the triple doctrine of being in favor of themselves, being against the other superpower and all it stands for, and willing to express this in action, up to and including nuclear holocaust, destructive both of themselves and of their allies.[21]

Now, to summarize the whole argument:

1. The Second World War had two theaters, the Atlantic and the Pacific, leaving out only South America, Africa except for the northern rim, and South Asia. The Cold War has two theaters that are prefigured by the Second World War: the Atlantic and Pacific theaters. Much of the rest of the world is organized in the same way, but less clearly so. The Pacific theater is less crystallized than the Atlantic theater, partly because of the asymmetry in the roles played by the two superpowers, partly because domestic issues are more salient, partly because Oriental logic may tolerate more ambiguity.

2. To clarify by contrast: the leading nonaligned country in the world, India, may serve as an example of the opposite type of policy. The country was divided in 1947 into intolerant Moslem Pakistan, and religiously highly tolerant and mixed India (although with a clear Hindu majority). Pakistan was enrolled in the Western camp (the now defunct CENTO system) together with Turkey and Iran; India was not. India could have joined the Soviet camp, but it did not. If it had, the United States would probably have mobilized all surrounding countries even more eagerly, creating European and East Asian conditions also in South Asia. As it stands now, the relationships to the ASEAN countries have strong military connotations, directly or

indirectly, but less so than in the two major arenas. Glory to India for keeping out of this!

3. Peacelessness and maldevelopment go together, hand in hand. There is a two-track program everywhere: hostility and military mobilization without and within, even with highly offensive arms in the name of peace, and imitation of specific aspects of the models set by the superpowers in the name of development. But the militarization resulting from the first part of this program puts its stamp on the development effort. Development becomes centralized, bureaucratic, and if not in all details imitative, at least not critical of the protective superpower. And those very patterns of development, giving power and privilege to capitalist entrepreneurial elites and to socialist party elites, increase the tensions further, tightening the alliance between nonmilitary and military elites, with the civilians working for the military effort and the military promising to protect them against the anger of the population.

In short, grossly deformed societies appear in both camps, in both theaters—a heavy price to be paid not only by this generation but by generations to come. In Western Europe the anger takes the form of peace movement struggle against the nuclear holocaust. In Eastern Europe it takes the form of the struggle against repression, for democracy against party dictatorship, for human rights, and for economic decentralization. In capitalist Southeast/East Asia it takes the form of struggle against repression and misery to survive in the face of flagrant inequality and blatant exploitation. In socialist East Asia it takes the form of struggle against repression, against the monotony and lack of dynamism of the socialist system after the basic needs have been satisfied. The basic question remains: Where does all this lead us?

ON THE FUTURE OF THE COLD WAR

The basic conclusions to be drawn from Figure 1 and Table 1 are that the total inter- and intra-national structure is extremely strong, well woven together in a solid, generalized Cold War manifesting itself in two basic theaters of the world. They are, at the same time, the points of gravity of the world economic system—another reason for the strong interconnection between the issues of peace and war and the issues of development and maldevelopment. By and large, the actors

have been doing their jobs, issuing the appropriate ideological signals, following the organizational blueprints for capitalist and socialist development, respectively, inside the countries, and for polarized
conflict behavior without.

The situation is even worse. More of the world is also enrolled in
the structure. The generalized Cold War has a South American theater[22] with such heavy components as the Rio de Janeiro treaty system, Cuba and Nicaragua, the tremendous efforts to align and train
the South American military all over the continent,[23] and so on.
Africa is also partly being enrolled, in this case perhaps due more to
Soviet efforts, assisted by Cuba, although also for special Cuban reasons; such as a sense of missionary zeal and responsibility, being the
first Third World country to go socialist and for that reason making it
more difficult for others to do so. The watchdog was awake. In addition, much of the Cuban population hails from Africa, and partly
from the southwestern coast. West Asia has been crystallized for a
long time by (as is also the case for Africa) two particularly malignant
tumors left behind by the collapsing British Empire: South Africa
and Israel, contributing to the Cold War with their own conflict energies, pitting races and ethnic groups against each other.

We now face four questions: Can this structure/process be coun-
teracted at all? Are these actors also writing the future script, or has
the script already been written and they are merely playing their
roles, more or less well? In the latter case, who wrote the script? And,
are the actors capable of leaving the show?

The way I have interpreted that script is relatively global and relatively wholistic. That approach has the advantage of making interconnections across geographical borders and across such disciplines as
peace studies and development studies more transparent. But it has
the disadvantage of making everything hang almost too well together, with seamless webs, so that the obvious conclusion, a major world
nuclear war, releasing all that emotional and organizational energy
piling up on both sides, seems inescapable.

We certainly do not want that conclusion even if it is rational, dic-
tated by reason; and even if drifting toward such a war seems confirmed by newspaper headlines practically speaking every day. And
yet, not only the fear of that war but also human reason lead to the
obvious conclusion that there will be counterforces. Precisely because
there is a process of such grandiose dimensions in the wrong direc-

tion, there will also be a *reactio* to all this. The points of action for peace are obvious, using again the logic shown in Table 1:

1. *In the victorious countries:* their self-righteousness, by pointing to less than idealistic motivations in connection with the Second World War; their traumas, by trying to cure them (not easy); their development programs, by pointing out their flaws, planting seeds of doubt; their conflict, by making it look not only dangerous but also ludicrous.

2. *In the defeated countries:* absolving them of their humiliation; insisting that the Second World War is long past; trying to cure them of their traumas (again, not so easy); criticizing their client behavior in imitating superpower development programs; stimulating more autonomous forces; making the conflict look not only dangerous and ridiculous, but their own behavior in that conflict an act of utter submission and servility inviting disaster.

3. *As to the ideologies:* criticizing them as neither excluding each other (how about social democracy?) nor spanning the ideological universe (how about green wave ideologies?); trying to escape from the liberalism/marxism false dichotomy, from the negativism of anti-communism and anti-imperialism; criticizing the "enemy of my friend is my enemy" and "the enemy of my enemy is my friend" logic by pointing to the ambiguities, the complexities, of the real world defying such simplistic conflict logic; being more imaginative in connection with development programs.

4. *As to divided countries:* doing everything possible to bring them closer together, if not necessarily in the form of complete reunification; paying the exit price for decoupling from superpowers in the currency of neutrality and defensive military preparedness (there is security to be gained from such arrangements), not with nuclear proliferation (although it may be said that this was, possibly, the price India also paid for her remarkable stance mentioned above; the glory has radioactive spots).

5. *As to the alliance systems:* The problem is probably more what kind of military doctrine they have than their existence. Change that military doctrine from offensive to defensive, let the alliances be exercises in peace-making, not in preparation for war.[24]

6. *The most faithful countries:* See that they gradually change their roles and recognize that the Second World War is over, that vic-

torious and defeated countries alike should now graduate from the
Second World War logic. For the defeated countries this means re-
emergence in full autonomy without invoking the ghost of the past,
meaning militarism for both Germany and Japan (not so easy both to
reject the past and have faith in the future).

7. *The unfaithful countries, protest countries:* See that more of
them emerge, as many as possible. On the other hand, the question
is how to do this without invoking not only the anger of the superpowers (this is automatic) but their fear, to the point that they strike
out, not only against the protest countries, but also against the other
side, in the hope that conflict without might bring in its wake soli-
darity and loyalty within. It should be remembered that both superpowers have an image of what a normal client country is. A normal
country is willing to be subservient not only in terms of following
superpower (military) command and imitating its program, but also
to the point of being at its disposal as a "theater" for a holocaust in
the name of the struggle of Good against Evil. This is the solid basis
on which popular movements can build, gradually eroding the tie
between their elites and the superpowers—a process which probably
has already gone a long way throughout the system, in both camps,
in both theaters—only the erosion process is not yet sufficiently visible.[25]

8. *Independent countries:* See that more are produced, that they
align themselves as nonaligned countries in order to become more
visible, regardless of how contradictory such formulas may sound.
Will New Zealand become an example—and in that case followed by
whom in the Pacific or the Atlantic theaters?

This list looks like a relatively systematic catalogue of the night-
mares of superpowers and client country elites, at the same time list-
ing hopes of the many movements working against the Cold War
structure/process. And that immediately raises a problem: Is there
one point on the list, or underlying this list, that is more important
than all others? An Archimedean point from which the Cold War system may be altered?

I doubt that very much. I think they are all important, although
not necessarily equally important. The advantage of a wholistic analysis is precisely that it makes one see the interconnection between so
many issues that are treated in a more separate manner in a more

atomistic approach. And the conclusion in terms of *actio* is obvious: millions of human beings acting on all these points at the same time in parallel, synchronic fashion, in both camps, in both theaters, so that the total energy becomes considerable even if the *reactio* looks very modest at any single point, and at any single point in time.

Of course, we might develop the theory that all of the Cold War comes from the superpowers, and that two popular revolts, one in each country, and simultaneously, might change them. This may be the case. But the counterarguments against that type of reasoning are rather heavy. The processes would have to be truly simultaneous, which is highly unlikely, otherwise one party might take advantage of the weakening of the other. Gorbachev's initiatives are essentially unilateral; the United States/NATO might take advantage of that. Consequently, I advance the case for parallel action everywhere, which means that the peace/development forces would have to be at least as well coordinated as the peacelessness/maldevelopment forces.

There is no basis in what has just been said for excessive optimism. Just as the Cold War process engenders antiprocesses, antiprocesses will also lead in turn to their *reactio,* in terms of efforts to solidify and reinforce, the Cold War process. There is so much vested interest in the process. Ideological consensus in alliances may be threatened, and that may serve as a stimulus for the superpowers to reinforce their command, whipping dissidents into line. The career patterns of countries, from faithful via unfaithful to independent, may be reversed, and not only due to superpower pressure, but for purely internal reasons. The peace movement in one theater may find sources of inspiration in the other theaters because they are so structurally similar; this structural similarity may then become a causal factor. But that also works for the peacelessness movement.[26] Submissiveness in one theater may lead to submissiveness in the other: "There, you see, it does not work; we can just as well give in." And one or both of the leaders of the leading countries may at some point come to the conclusion that now is the time to strike, to get rid of all this irritating subversiveness by launching the Big War. A factor that might make for some caution in the peace and development movements would be the admonition: do not act too quickly, do not demand too much.

And yet the peace forces are there, like billions of ants, even termites, gnawing at something that looks very impressive, very solid.

So, maybe one day the tenants of that structure will decide to vacate it, move out before it all crumbles, falls on their heads and kills them, creating a structure/process for peace and development instead? With things running the way they are, that day should come sooner rather than later.

Addendum: Alternative Security Policies in the Pacific Theater

In my book *There Are Alternatives!*[27] a general theory is presented with concrete policy suggestions in the field of alternative security policies. The basic idea is to conceive of the security of a country in terms of a combination of high capacity for defensive defense (as opposed to offensive defense[28] or no defense at all) and a high level of invulnerability. Then, defensive defense is seen in terms of two dimensions: the autonomous, nationally based capability of defending the national territory (including territorial waters and territorial air space) with any combination of conventional military defense, paramilitary defense, and nonmilitary defense; *and,* on the other hand, decoupling from military alliances with countries that base their defense on highly offensive doctrines—in particular those of superpowers. In practice the latter means leaning toward, or achieving, nonalignment, but not necessarily neutralism in any ideological sense, which in any case might be better than being a client country.

Correspondingly, invulnerability also divides into two dimensions: the inner strength of the country in terms of economic self-reliance (meaning capacity for self-sufficiency in basics even in times of war, and trade on an equitable basis beyond that), ecological balance in the country as an ecosystem, social cohesion, and political autonomy. And, on top of that, the type of invulnerability that does not derive from the inner strength just described, but from the outer usefulness to both or all sides in conflicts by having reasonable relations with everybody.

In Table 2 the reader will find an effort to assess the situation of the Pacific theater, from the point of view of twelve actors or groups of actors located on the littoral or in the Pacific itself. The numbers given, 0, 1, and 2, are "grades": 0 being the lowest, meaning no use-

Table 2. Alternative Security Policies in the Pacific Theater*

Actor	Defensive Defense	Decoupling from Superpowers	Inner Strength	Outer Usefulness	TOTAL
USA	0	0	1	0(1/2)	1(1/2)
Canada	1	0	1	0	2
South America	2	0	0	0	2
Australia	1	0	0	0	1
New Zealand	2	1	0	0	3
Pacific Islands	2	1	1	1	5
ASEAN	2	0	0	0	2
Mini-Japans/Chinas	1	0	0	0	1
Socialist East Asia	1	0	1	0	2
Japan	2	0	0	0	2
China	1	1	1	1	4
Soviet Union	0	0	1	0(1/2)	1(1/2)
TOTAL	15	3	6	2(3)	26(27)

* For key to rankings see text.

ful development along this dimension, 2 meaning "very satisfactory," and 1 being in between. Needless to say, these judgments are very subjective and should not be taken too seriously. They only serve as background for highlighting some issues in the Pacific theater.

The situation is very bleak, particularly as compared with the situation in the Atlantic theater, where in Europe there are a number of countries that score high in this type of exercise. Thus, Switzerland gets a full house, 8; then follow Yugoslavia and Albania with 6 each; and then Finland and Austria both with 5; and Sweden and Malta with 4; a total of seven countries. Among them three countries—conservative Switzerland, radical Albania, and in-between Yugoslavia—indicate that alternative security options are open for countries of all colors. And Finland, Austria, and Sweden are old, tested models.

An outstanding characteristic of the Pacific theater is precisely this: there is no model country. The highest score in this presentation is given to the Pacific Islands, where whatever defense there is cannot possibly be seen as offensive or provocative, but in that case by default rather than by design. There is also some vague alignment, and by implication some weak nonalignment. There is some inner strength, and there is—particularly recently in connection with the fisheries—some symmetry in outer usefulness.[29]

The Pacific Islands comprise many very small islands, among them some very small countries.[30] They are exposed to tremendous pressure from the dominant country in the region, the United States. Then, one outside power, France, shows its contempt for the indigenous population by continued atomic testing in the area, as well as denial of independence to one of the bigger islands. And, on top of this there is also the power of the Soviet Union, although (so far) in a modest role. In short, whatever peace policy they might engage in, these small countries are highly vulnerable. The "5" in the table might easily change downward to considerably lower grades.

Next in line is China. Certainly not entirely defensive given its nuclear arms, but then those weapons seem to be deployed within a doctrine that is more defensive. China is certainly not entirely decoupled today, leaning more to the United States; it no longer has the same inner strength as before, as China is becoming increasingly trade dependent; and China still has a good distance to go in order to make the economic relations and other relations more symmetric (but that may change quickly).[31] However, there is something peculiar about China. The most populous country in the world, it still seems sometimes as if the country is not in this world at all; in a sense this is not strange, given its traditional self-perception as the country located between heaven and earth.[32]

Third in line is New Zealand under the present stewardship of Prime Minister David Lange, who seems to operate within a military doctrine of defensive defense, and to a large extent through nuclear nonalignment, decoupled from the superpowers (how much so still remains to be seen).[33] But the country is heavily trade dependent, and far from symmetric in its international relations. Also, some of the comments that apply to the Pacific Islands would also apply here. The posture is vulnerable, easily subject to change.

Thus, the total situation, as mentioned, is rather bleak. Perhaps we see it particularly clearly by looking at the bottom line of the table. The total sum is only 26. Ideally it should have been 96—a "peace fulfillment," according to this index, of only 27%. There is some inclination toward defensive defense. But given the low level of decoupling and the low level of inner strength and outer usefulness, the comment stated above applies: peace is by default rather than by design. Weak actors, all of them. And with the exception of Mongolia/North Korea/Vietnam/Laos/Kampuchea—and the Soviet Union of course—one way or the other under the dominion of the United States. Except—China?

Let us speculate a little about a more desirable situation. Let us assume that the two superpowers will not change their roles in the Pacific theater for the foreseeable future although they may develop more symmetric trade relations (as indicated with the hopeful "1/2" in the table). But let us imagine that China comes out in the open, as the biggest actor population-wise in the theater, with a completely defensive military doctrine, a strong policy of nonalignment in theory as well as in practice, and friendly relations with both superpowers at the same time (not some type of balance over time, being friendly to only one of them or neither of them at the same time). Let us further imagine that the "trade friction" between Japan and the United States leads Japan in the direction of decoupling from the United States, to more self-reliance and more ability to trade with both sides in the Cold War. And let us then imagine, on top of all of this, that a course of action of that type is followed by the mini-Japans/Chinas of South Korea, Taiwan, Hong Kong, and Singapore, and the mini-Soviet Unions of Mongolia, North Korea, Vietnam/Laos/Kampuchea. Moreover, that the Pacific Islands and New Zealand manage to keep the position they have achieved, and also to get Australia with them, up from "1" to at least "3" or "4."

In that case the whole picture would certainly look different. Between the two superpowers there would be a vast cushion of countries with an array of different policies, able to absorb in a creative manner a number of different conflicts without getting closer to a warlike situation. The situation would be more "messy" for fighting a war, considerably better for building a peace precisely because it is messy.[34]

In saying this, nothing particular is expected from South America. These regimes are deeply engulfed in their own domestic problems, seeing international relations almost uniquely in terms of relations with the United States, not yet having discovered in any significant sense the rest of the Pacific theater. And Canada is a minor actor in this connection, participating in military exercises but so far not projecting much independent thinking or initiative in the direction of the Pacific.

In short, the hope would come from the western, Asian, side of the Pacific or from the Pacific countries themselves, including New Zealand and Australia. And at this point a major difficulty immediately becomes apparent. The countries are not only small but also so disparate, so far away from each other geographically, culturally, socially, economically, politically, and militarily. If I should make a conjecture, I would not expect too much from Australia or New Zealand beyond what the latter has already done, nor from the Pacific Islands because of their vulnerability. This means that I would pin my hopes on the lower half of the table rather than on the upper half. ASEAN is today a very important community of nations, 270 million strong, and might one day discover the advantage of also having the socialist Second World as a trade partner, particularly when the United States becomes less able to absorb goods produced elsewhere. The same would apply to the mini-Japans/Chinas and, as mentioned already, to Japan and China.

In other words, the key to the relationship lies in East Asia, not in the Pacific theater as such. An East Asia less mesmerized by the United States, with a less paranoid and less domineering Soviet Union to the north, might develop new relationships that would provide the whole Pacific theater with a new, more interesting configuration,[35] and above all, with a configuration having a much higher peace potential than the dangers we are confronting at the present, with submarines from both sides increasingly getting entangled with each other. And also a higher development potential, based on economic independence (self-reliance) and interdependence ("outer usefulness") rather than classical dependence on a big "partner."

CHAPTER 3

Peace and Development in the Pacific Hemisphere: A Conflict Map and Some Proposals

To what extent is the Pacific hemisphere a peaceful hemisphere? We very well know that in the past it has not been as peaceful as the name should indicate. The Pacific war of 1931–45, with Japan alone against practically everybody else except South America, was devastating.[1] The aftermath of that war is still with us. And before that we had the "discoveries," meaning essentially Western imperialism colonizing practically everything in the Pacific Islands and the western and eastern rims, with the exception of China, Japan (and Thailand). Peaceful? Certainly not when the past is considered.

But what about the present? There is no war going on in the area right now (1988); could that not be a hopeful sign? Of course it all depends on how "peace" is defined, and it will be defined here as absence of any major direct violence and any major structural violence. Skirmishes there will always be; some amount of repression and exploitation there will also always be. We are looking for major cases. And we would include under "direct violence" also threats of direct violence because of some major direct conflict in the area. "Structural violence" is another expression for repression and exploitation built into a structure, and in this case we are focusing on international structures. Structural conflicts are included not only because they might one day translate into direct conflict, with direct violence, but also because they are violent in their own right.

To this should then be added one more consideration: how basic the conflict is. I would not leave the definition of that term to governments with their national interests. Rather, I would say that basic conflicts involve basic human needs. And I see four classes of basic human needs: for survival; for a minimum of economic well-being;

for freedom; and for identity, or meaning in life.[2] These terms can be made more clear by mentioning their negations. The negation of survival is obviously death; the negation of economic well-being is misery (which may lead to a slow death); the negation of freedom is repression; and the negation of identity/meaning is alienation.

Our century has witnessed giant versions of these negations: the mega-death of the Holocaust; the mega-misery currently going on in the Third World, aptly referred to by George Kent as the silent holocaust; the mega-repression known as KZ or Gulag; and the mega-alienation that is less known and less discussed but could be referred to as spiritual death. Deprive a person in particular, and a whole people in general, of their identity—for instance by forcing upon them another religion, another language, another style of life—and spiritual death may set in. What may be seen as liberation, even salvation, by the colonizers (engaged in cultural colonization in this case) may be seen as the extreme of repression by the colonized. And spiritual death may then, in turn, be translated into somatic death because of a lack of desire to continue living. The translation mechanism is not necessarily suicide, but insufficient attention to what is needed to keep going, to survive.

It is with yardsticks such as these that I am now looking at the Pacific hemisphere. I do not expect to find the mega-phenomena going on right now. But I do expect to find the threat of direct violence and actual exercise of structural violence. However, to explore these threats we have to be systematic, starting with a clear image of what is meant by the Pacific hemisphere.

Being located in Hawaii I would divide the Pacific hemisphere into four parts, with subdivisions:

1. The Pacific Rim
   a. Eastern rim in the Americas
   b. Western rim in Asia
2. The Pacific Islands (Basin)
3. The Pacific Polar Regions
   a. Arctic
   b. Antarctic
4. The Pacific hub: Hawaii

Concerning the fourth part of this division, Hawaii, perhaps nobody else in the Pacific hemisphere would agree. But let people in Hawaii be permitted to entertain the illusion of being the hub in a basin surrounded by a rim!

It should be noted that I put the word "Basin" in parentheses above. Not only does the expression seem too "wet" to serve as a basis for describing highly concrete politics; it might also be indicative of old-fashioned geopolitical thinking. Any limitation of the Pacific hemisphere to "Asia and the Pacific" in the sense of traditional spheres of influence of the United States of America, referring to the totality as "the Pacific Basin," should of course not be taken seriously. What should be taken seriously is the tremendous amount of interaction between the western and eastern rims of the Pacific, the increasing significance of the Pacific Islands, and the potential significance of Hawaii being geographically located in the middle, being multiethnic, and being a bridgehead to the United States. Hence "Pacific hemisphere" for the totality and forget about the "basin."

Thus, obviously, Central and South America belong to the Pacific hemisphere even if geopolitically they may be handled by Washington in a "Western Hemisphere" context. Equally obviously, the Soviet Union, with the longest shoreline of all the countries bordering on the Pacific, also belongs to the hemisphere even if it is handled by Washington in an "East-West" context. That does not identify all of the Soviet Union as belonging to the Pacific. Maybe "Siberia" would be a suitable qualifier, or the "East Coast," leaving to the Soviet Union to define what that would mean. Similarly, the U.S. mainland does not in its entirety belong to the Pacific hemisphere, calling for the same exercise usually settled in favor of the expression "West Coast." The same would apply, obviously, to China and to Canada.

Based on these reflections we get the following actors in the Pacific hemisphere:

1a. *The Eastern Rim of the Pacific,* which would include Canada (West Coast), United States of America (West Coast), México, Central America (Guatemala, El Salvador, Honduras, Nicaragua, Costa Rica—to this group we could add Panamá although that is not quite correct), South America, (Colombia, Ecuador, Peru, Bolivia—which until relatively recently was a Pacific west coast state—Chile).

1b. *The Western Rim of the Pacific,* including the Soviet Union (east coast); China (east coast); Japan; the mini-Japans/Chinas (South Korea, Taiwan, Hong Kong, Singapore); Socialist East Asia

(Mongolia, North Korea, Vietnam, Laos, Kampuchea, and perhaps also Burma); and Southeast Asia (Philippines, Indonesia, Malaysia, Thailand, Brunei, and Singapore once more).

2. *The Pacific Islands,* which would include Micronesia (Guam, the Northern Marianas, Palau, the Federated States of Micronesia, the Marshall Islands, Kiribati, and Nauru); Polynesia (Tuvalu, Tokelau Island, Fiji, Wallis and Futuna, Western Samoa, American Samoa, Tonga, Niue, Cook Islands, French Polynesia, Pitcairn Island, and Easter Island); Melanesia (Papua New Guinea, Solomon Islands, Vanuatu, and New Caledonia); Australia; New Zealand.

3. *The Pacific Polar Regions:* Arctic, Antarctic.

4. And then there is, again, the vantage point from which all these observations are made: *Hawaii,* traditionally a part of Polynesia, at present a state of the United States of America.

We now have to simplify to the following list of actors: United States, Canada, South America (Mexico, Central and South America as commonly said), the Pacific Islands (all three groups), New Zealand/Australia, Southeast Asia, Socialist Asia, mini-Japans/Chinas, Japan, China, Soviet Union. That gives us a total of eleven actors. To that could be added an actor number 12 which plays a considerable and very harmful role in the Pacific hemisphere, although not being a part of it: France. However, it being *in* the Pacific hemisphere but not *of* it we shall leave France aside and make only some comments in that connection, thus not dignifying French colonialism by adding its name to the list of Pacific hemisphere actors.

I do not think it possible to collapse this list—a compromise between too little and too much diversity—any further.

Since we are now heading for an 11 × 11 matrix with 55 "interactor" relationships to examine, the question is what to put inside the matrix. (See Table 3.) The first and obvious distinction is simply in terms of "+" for good, harmonious, positive relationship; 0 for mutual irrelevance, and "−" for negative, conflict-loaded relationship. The latter is then divided into "(D)" for direct conflict and "(S)" for structural conflict. Later on we might like to qualify conflicts in terms of "low," "medium," "high," and even quantify this by using numerals—all the time with a minus sign in front. From the table we can get some crude information about the conflict situation in the Pacific hemisphere. Let us here engage in some commentary.

We start with the United States of America, a major actor in the

Table 3. A Conflict Map for the Pacific Hemisphere

	U.S.	Canada	South America	Pacific Islands	N. Z./ Australia	Southeast Asia	Socialist East Asia	Mini-Jpn./ Chinas	Japan	China	Soviet Union	-	+
U. S.	X	- (S)	- (S,D)	- (S)	-, + (S)	-, + (S,D)	- (D)	- (S)	- (S,D)	-, + (S)	-, (D)	10	3
Canada		X	+	+	+	+	-, + (D)	+	-, + (S)	+	-, +	4	9
South America			X	O	O	O	O	O	-, (S)	O	O	2	1
Pacific Islands				X	-, + (S)	O	O	O	-, + (S,D)	O	O	3	3
N. Z./ Australia					X	-, +	-, +	-, +	-, + (S,D)	O	O	6	7
Southeast Asia						X	-, (D)	+	-, + (S,D)	-, +	-, (D)	6	6
Socialist East Asia							X	+	-, (D)	-, (D)	+	7	3
Mini-Jpn./ Chinas								X	-, + (S,D)	-, (D)	-, (D)	6	4
Japan									X	-, (D,S)	-, (D)	10	5
China										X	-, (D,S)	6	3
Soviet Union											X	6	2

Pacific hemisphere and also a major carrier of conflicts. The relation
U.S.-Canada has been shown as a minus, which may be a surprise for
some Americans, but not for many Canadians. Is the 49th parallel a
border of peace? Yes, in the sense that not only are no shots fired but
there is no exchange of threats, no arms race, and so on. But there is a
massive U.S. penetration into Canada, controlling well above 70% of
the Canadian economy, turning Canada into a military client and for
all practical purposes into a political satellite. Added to this comes a
considerable amount of cultural penetration, except in French Canada where the language serves as an efficient barrier against which the
United States is relatively helpless.

All of this, of course, is much more strongly developed in the relations *U.S.-South America,* one of the strongest cases of penetration
and structural violence in general in the world today. One reason for
this is the nature of the bridgehead of U.S. imperialism in South
America; the structure left behind by Iberian colonialism over almost
the whole area. Spain and Portugal did not have a "French Revolution" until very recently, in the 1970s, after the demise of the Franco
and Salazar regimes (and persons). The legacy left behind by Spanish
and Portuguese colonialism was a social formation run by what in
Spanish is aptly called *los poderes fácticos,* the real powers, as
opposed to people, presidents, cabinets, national assemblies, su-
preme courts, and so on. Instead, power is held by the church, the
landowners, and the military. In other words, the people traditionally
in control of normative power, economic power, and military power
—ideas, carrots, and sticks—respectively.

Add to that the rapidly growing private business sector, more often
than not wedded to patterns of U.S. capitalism one way or the other,
and a very strong, five-headed combination comes out in charge of
the total social formation. Not easy to stand up against that one. It
has happened successfully only twice in South American history:
Mexico 1910–11 and Cuba 1959. In both cases the process has been
met with the resistance of the United States for generations. That the
United States is also trying to stop the third effort to let a country be
handled more by its own population and less by *los poderes fácticos*
from inside and outside—in Nicaragua—goes without saying. Let it
only be mentioned that a fourth case, where the general model does
not hold true, is Costa Rica, a very special case due to peculiar historical and geographical circumstances. The result is, of course, one of
deeply entrenched conflict basically of the structural kind, with very

frequent directly violent outbursts of high or low intensity between the United States and South America.

The same holds for the *U.S.-Pacific Islands* relationship, except that in this case the military overtones sometimes become dominant. The social formations in the Pacific Islands are complex and the Spanish social model does not make much sense. The difference between American Samoa and Western Samoa is instructive. The United States is probably relatively firmly rooted in American Samoa, a phenomenon resented in Western Samoa. Yet it is quite evident that the structural conflict building up has well-known dimensions. A local upper class catering to U.S. military and economic interests crystallizes. To the Pacific Islander the U.S. mainland is seen as the center of one's own country, which, in turn, is seen as a hopeless periphery. And the only way this is prevented from exploding is a very old one: by bribing the population.

A characteristic of the Pacific Islands, as opposed to South America, is that the number of inhabitants is so low that bribing is possible. It is possible to buy 32,000 people (American Samoa), possible even for 160,000 (Western Samoa), but hardly possible to buy the millions living in a South American country. Consequently U.S. imperialism shows up in a much more brutal form in Latin America than in the Pacific Islands, relying on sticks rather than carrots: on direct military intervention; on indirect military intervention using other countries or other soldiers; on torturism and similar techniques inside the country, and so on. Paying the people who kill and destroy is cheaper than paying off the whole population.

What is the relationship *U.S.-New Zealand/Australia?* Positive to Australia for the time being, negative to New Zealand because New Zealand has refused to participate in the major system for possible exercise of direct violence, "nuclear deterrence." How this relationship will develop in the future is uncertain. Australia may go New Zealand's way; New Zealand may fall back to Australia's position; the United States may pull out of ANZUS or dismantle ANZUS for purely economic reasons. Who knows?

The relationship *U.S.-Southeast Asia* is very similar to the relationship with South America. Of course, this similarity shows up most clearly in the relationship with the Philippines, itself formerly colonized by Spain, itself dominated up until our day by that same pre-French-Revolution social formation, with *los poderes fácticos* in charge. As in South America the church is trying to have it both ways:

arguing a theology of liberation for the people, the masses; and arguing the old theology of repression for people higher up in society. There is even a division of labor inside the church for this purpose, a "low church" and a "high church"; an old tradition in Christianity.

When we come to Indonesia, it is enough to contemplate what happened in the mid-'60s, with the heavy U.S. responsibility for the blood-bath committed against the Chinese part of the population, suspected both of being communist and of planning a military coup. Relationships with Malaysia and Thailand are for the time being less fraught with such problems at the overt level. But the U.S. contributions to the (so far) successful fight against "communist" rebellions in northern Malaysia and northeast (also southwest) Thailand is of course very well known. On the other hand, relations with Brunei and Singapore are rather harmonious.

When we then come to the relations *U.S.-Socialist East Asia,* the picture becomes rather clear-cut. One of the most bloody wars not only of our century but of all times was raging between the United States and Vietnam, euphemistically dubbed the "Second Indochina War" (the first one being with France 1945–54; the United States then taking over until its defeat in 1975). Another war of about the same magnitude was fought essentially by the United States in Korea; a country so unjustly divided that what happened during 1950–53 was above all an effort to reunite the country, emanating from what was then the stronger, northern part. The effort failed.

Add to this U.S. bombardment of Laos and Kampuchea bordering on the genocidal, no doubt a major contributing factor in the Pol Pot genocide that took place later. The only thing remaining would be a relatively peaceful attitude to Mongolia, if for no other reason than because it is remote. Correspondingly, there is no structural conflict, as there is no direct relation at all. There can be little doubt as to the basic purpose of the United States in its relationships with these countries: to eliminate communism. In Africa communism may perhaps be permitted. But traditional areas of interest to the United States, such as South America (including Central America, Mexico, and the Caribbean), Southeast and East Asia and, of course, Europe should be *Kommunistenrein.*[3]

When we then move on to the relationships *U.S.-mini-Japans/ Chinas* we get into territory well known from contemporary debate. Officially this is formulated in terms of trade deficits, and not only relative to Japan but even relative to the mini-Japans. At the deeper level of analysis it is a question of how the whole international division of labor is changing, with even those small countries being able to come ahead of the United States in terms of the sophistication of the goods and services exchanged. All four regimes can be seen as firmly anticommunist and also as not having significant communist minorities. The basis for direct conflict, in other words, is not present. But the structural conflict is certainly there, and of considerable magnitude, this time with the United States in a new underdog role.

And that point holds, of course, even much more for the relationship *U.S.-Japan*. But there are also memories of a recent war of tragic and enormous proportions. That war ushered in the nuclear age, announcing not only the arrival on the military scene of a new type of weapon of mass destruction, but also the willingness to use it. I do not think it is far-fetched to assume that those particular experiences of August 6 and 9, 1945, are simmering deep down in the Japanese collective subconscious, as a fundamental trauma. In other words, the cycle of birth and rebirth of basic violence may be operating, searching for an occasion to manifest itself again. Which means that on top of a basic structural conflict there is also the material for a basic direct conflict as a carryover from the Pacific War, which in turn was a carryover from a succession of direct and structural conflicts preceding it. There is a *karma* to everything.

The relationship *U.S.-China* is more ambiguous. There are definitely cooperative elements, but equally definitely conflict elements. There is an old pattern of U.S. cultural (missionary—religious and educational), economic, political, and military cooperation with the elites in China. But there is also a deep U.S. suspiciousness of the Chinese masses, confirmed by everything Mao Zedong stood for particularly in the U.S. construction of him. This even went so far at the end of the 1960s that the Soviet Union was no longer seen as the major enemy of the United States of America. The major enemy was "Red China," "Mainland China." It consisted of "hordes," red/yellow, "swarming"—as evidenced by their behavior in the Korean War. The Cultural Revolution was exactly what one could expect from such people.

And yet it took only a tiny Chinese indication of readiness for negotiations to redefine the situation and make China graduate from its status as most evil country, MEC, to "most favored nation," MFN, in technical trade terms[4]—an amazing career, which certainly took place in the minds of Americans rather than in reality. But further down the road is probably the same structural relationship the United States entertains with Japan and the mini-Japans/Chinas: a structural conflict deriving from the international vertical division of labor with the United States at the bottom. This will happen when China really gets off the ground economically, that is, showing what its labor force of 600 million is capable of doing. And this may happen sooner rather than later.

But it is less likely to happen in the *U.S.-Soviet Union* relationship in the near future. Even with the most optimistic *perestroika* prognosis it does not seem likely that the Soviet Union will be able to mobilize a sufficient amount of skilled workers, capital, research, technologies, and people with managerial skill so as to outcompete the United States in division of labor. On the other hand, the direct conflict which was never fought but was always threatened, mutually, during all the years of the Cold War has left memories. However much the Cold War may have diminished in intensity, it is certainly not completely over, and the terrible weaponry not only remains but reproduces itself into new forms of weapons of mass destruction, with Star Wars gradually replacing nuclear arms (or so I assume to be the case).[5] Faced with that terrible threat, confidence does not easily take root, if for no other reason than because superpowers think they have to have super-weapons, and super-weapons somehow presuppose super-enemies against whom they could one day be used. The step from super-enemy to super-hatred is but a short one. Unpropitious.

Looking back at what has so far been said about the U.S. relationship with the rest of the Pacific hemisphere there is only one possible conclusion: it is ridden with conflict, from west to east, from north to south. Some points are brighter than the others, such as Australia, some of the Southeast Asian countries, some aspects of the relations to the mini-Japans/Chinas, the ambiguity relative to China. But no relationship can be said to be purely positive. *Pax americana* has its costs in conflict currencies; sooner or later they have to be paid.

The whole picture changes the moment we turn to *Canada*, number two in line of our actors. The relationship to South America is positive; to the Pacific Islands positive; to the other dominions, New Zealand and Australia, positive; to Southeast Asia positive; to Socialist East Asia not that positive, but not that negative either; to mini-Japans/Chinas positive; to Japan maybe potentially more mixed, for some of the same reasons that apply to the United States; to China very positive, summarized in the prophetic character of the Canadian doctor Norman Bethune. The relationship to the Soviet Union is perhaps more ambiguous, but not so much so as the relationship the United States entertains with that country. Of course, there are simple reasons for this. The United States is the point man; Canada is operating in the shadow of the United States. We cannot but come to the conclusion that Canada has inserted itself very well in the Pacific hemisphere, that Canada has a range of goodwill and positive relationships to draw upon that would make Canada a potential peacemaker for a more peaceful Pacific hemisphere—a challenge for Canadian diplomacy.

The moment we turn to *South America* this changes. Of course for one thing, South America is relatively isolated from the rest of the Pacific hemisphere. Its relationship is predominantly with the United States, meaning a negative one. The structural relationship to the mini-Japans/Chinas and to Japan is also negative, but in a different way from the relation to the United States. The United States is being deposed economically all over the Pacific hemisphere by Japan, and increasingly by the mini-Japans/Chinas; South America is only changing imperialist power. The United States is entering a qualitatively new relationship in its position in the world; South America is remaining where it was, only changing its master (like Southeast Asia). It may even take some time before this is fully realized, including by the intellectuals of South America, accustomed as they are to identifying imperialism in particular and dominion in general with the great neighbor to the north. In addition, both China and the Soviet Union are so remote that neither direct nor structural relationships of any particular importance exist. The same applies, of course, to Socialist East Asia, Southeast Asia, New Zealand/Australia, and to the Pacific Islands.

If we now switch from the rim of the Pacific to the *Pacific Islands* we can better appreciate the unhappy situation in which they find themselves. They have been the colonial subjects of two major Pacific Rim countries, the United States and Japan. In addition they have been the colonial subjects of three major European powers: England, France, and Germany. And as if this were not enough, they have also had what in practice is colonial status (trusteeship) under New Zealand and Australia. They have been claimed, invaded, conquered, exploited, not only by neighbors but also by those from very far away; not only by the big, but also by the small.[6] Of course that sets a pattern for a negative relationship, based on the memories of the distant past (although some of them may be positive), and also the memories of the very near past when the colonizers were resisting giving up what they had. Also there are memories of the present, with some colonial powers continuing, with various means, to hold on to their power. In fact, the United States still holds on to American Samoa, France still holds on to French Polynesia and New Caledonia; England still holds on to Pitcairn; even little Chile, to Easter Island, and New Zealand and Australia also, to some islands. And neocolonialism, with "compacts" and all kinds of nonautonomous status, is not less problematic, making for ambiguous relations also to such small powers as New Zealand and Australia.

Logically this would mean potentially good relationships with those on the Pacific Rim who do not share with the islands a past and recent history of that kind. The moment there is the rumor of a fisheries agreement between the Soviet Union and Fiji, the warning signals go up in the old colonial powers: What is the real purpose? Are they heading for a military base in the Fiji Islands? Behind these warning signals we find, of course, a combination of awareness of how badly the "West" has treated the Pacific Islands, and fear that the islanders will now turn their backs on the West and embrace not only the non-West but even the anti-West. But the issue cannot be analyzed in such terms. The permissible U.S. media discourse is only in terms of dubious and devious Soviet intentions and behavior.

Since the Soviet Union lays itself bare to such accusations, the field should then, in principle, be relatively open for China which does not have an expansionist tradition into noncontiguous territory. The same should apply to the mini-Japans/Chinas, Southeast Asia, and Socialist East Asia. But not to Japan herself, who is very active in the area (particularly in the Marianas, and in Micronesia in general), and also bears a very heavy burden of extreme violence from the recent past, as well as a tendency to establish structural relationships of dominance, although in a more subtle way than the United States is able to do. In a corresponding vein, the field should be relatively open for Canada and South America, not to mention, of course, for a maximum of cooperation among the Pacific Islands groups themselves. But these are potentials only. The basic point about the situation of the Pacific Islands is their present isolation, their unhappy past, their uncertain future, and the blandness of their relations with the vast masses of lands surrounding them at a considerable distance.

The same cannot be said about *New Zealand/Australia*. They

entertain ambiguous relations to the United States, positive relations to Canada, bland relations to South America, ambiguous relations to the Pacific Islands, and ambiguous relations between themselves, of a type very similar to the relations between the United States and Canada, between England and Ireland, Sweden and Norway, Argentina and Chile—in short Big Brother, Small Brother relations. But none of that is serious.

The relationship *New Zealand/Australia-Southeast Asia* is more problematic, particularly when one looks at the sore point of over-populated Indonesia having as a close neighbor underpopulated Australia. And in this there is a solid ethnic factor which may become more and more important also in the relationship to the Pacific Islands. Today New Zealand is also being judged in terms of how it treats the Maori (and Samoan and Tongan) local population, Australia in terms of how it treats the Australian Aborigines. For Australia of the bicentenary the judgment is catastrophic. Indonesia itself has a bad record relative to the Pacific Islands because of Irian Jaya. But Indonesia may some day turn Australia's bad record to its own advantage.

The relationship *New Zealand/Australia-Socialist East Asia* is also somewhat problematic. Although the United States was by far the major belligerent against the socialist countries, both New Zealand and Australia were relatively easily enrolled in the anticommunist cause acted out in Korea 1950–53 and in Vietnam 1965–75. It is difficult to assess how much remains of that conflict. Probably not very much, probably not more than could easily be healed with good diplomacy and positive relations. But the experience should not be repeated.

The relationships *New Zealand/Australia* have with *Japan* and with the *mini-Japans/Chinas* are, however, more problematic again. Here we are entering the same structural ground that was touched on above. Like Canada, New Zealand and Australia would have a position somewhere intermediate between the United States and South America. They are not deposed as leading economic powers by rising economic powers. Nor are they just changing masters in a relationship of essentially economic imperialism. It is more that they are reorienting themselves, getting used to a totally new context, neither close to the United States nor close to Europe in general and England in particular, whence they came originally. It is not necessarily a relationship loaded with conflict, although it could be. Several things seem to indicate that particularly between Japan and Australia the relationship might one day become very problematic, given the Japanese effort to include (parts of) Australia in the *dai-to-a kyoeiken* (the Greater East Asia Co-prosperity Sphere).[7]

With *China* and the *Soviet Union* it is hard to see that Australia and New Zealand have any immediate problem, particularly not with the Soviet Union. This was also the conclusion drawn by New Zealand's Prime Minister David Lange when he launched his epoch-making nuclear policy. If New Zealand had been located geographically between Washington and London, then perhaps he might have entertained the geopolitical perspectives of Washington and London; New Zealand is, however, south of Suva, in the South Pacific—a strong argument.[8] In other words, there is potential here for a very positive relationship with both big powers even if at present the relationship is relatively bland.

Moving now to *Southeast Asia,* a major factor in the foreign policies of these countries, as also for the mini-Japans/Chinas, is their anticommunism. The United States is their friend where direct conflict is concerned, but the relationship is much more complicated when structural relations are considered. More particularly, the Southeast Asian countries are increasingly turning away from the United States as a trading partner, toward Japan and the mini-Japans/Chinas. This will make for some conflict with the United States, but nothing relative to the structural conflict they willingly if not knowingly are courting in their relationship with their powerful neighbor to the north, Japan. And in this case the memories of the past will remain with the countries for a generation or two, the atrocities being of such magnitude that they are not easily wiped out by the positive memories of Japan setting the stage for liberation from Western colonialism.

In the past, the major organizing axis, anticommunism, expressed itself not only in enlisting U.S. aid in suppressing "internal" communism, but also in staving off the perceived or pretended threat from China and the Soviet Union. However, China and the Soviet Union are rapidly changing character, not only in being less bent on stimulating socialist revolutions in other countries but also in the sense of developing new social experiments—with increased trade in more interesting products as one important implication. Both Southeast Asia and the mini-Japans/Chinas will probably develop more positive relationships with both of them.

This may be watched with considerable chagrin by the United

States, but there is very little the United States can do about it. Both China and the Soviet Union are probably heading for a major explosion in economic growth the moment they manage to bring capital, technology, and better management to bear on their enormous resources in terms of nature and labor—resources that, in addition, through socialism are put at the total disposal of the economy.[9] The countries have gotten rid of the shackles of capitalism and are now trying to get rid of the shackles of socialism. It will still take some time before the shackles of capitalism reappear. There is an open window for both of them to make good use of. The Soviet Union is industrially more developed, and China is more dynamic.

How does *Socialist East Asia* insert itself in this picture? It is negative to the United States, ambiguous to the dominions; essentially negative to Japan and to the mini-Japans/Chinas, having been exposed to the former and scaring the latter; negative to Southeast Asia, which is also scared and in addition has the (understandable!) Vietnam invasion of Kampuchea in the neighborhood. Relations with the Soviet Union, however, should be relatively positive, except for Mongolia. But China is Confucian-Buddhist. My bet is on China.

And that brings us toward the end of the list of fifty-five relationships. At the end we have the absolutely crucial *Japan–China–Soviet Union* triangle. And how this one is going to develop in the future is not easy to say.

Of course, the memory of atrocious direct violence in the recent past committed by Japan in China is weighing heavily. So is the memory of Soviet "social imperialism" and the border conflicts. So are the memories of the Russo-Japanese war of 1904–05, of Japanese participation in the interventionist wars of 1918–22, of the Soviet attack on Japan in the last week of the Pacific war. So is the fear in China of a structural conflict with Japan that might evolve in a very negative direction. But the three parties have been able to keep all these grievances within bounds, in a sense even admirably so. The relations are negative, and the Japanese insistence on textbook revision does not help; and that also applies to the relationship between Japan and the other three actors in East Asia. But it could have been much worse. It was very bad historically, is not *very* bad today, possibly will be much better tomorrow.

The relationship between Japan and the Soviet Union has a built-in negative element. Feelings are crystallizing to some extent around the "Northern Territories" or the "South Kuril Islands," depending on the angle from which they are seen. There is also the heavy problem of what a deeper engagement of Japan in the Soviet Union might imply in terms of structural conflict in the future. Will Japan also end up buying Siberia?

But the basic question mark in the whole area is, of course, the relationship between the two giants, China and the Soviet Union. And here we have little basis for any prediction. How two giant countries that have had recent socialist experience and are now developing mixed economies and world trade relations will relate to each other we simply do not know. All we know is that the relationship that they develop will have a heavy impact on the rest of the Pacific hemisphere, not to mention on the whole world. There is a history of recent direct conflict (Ussuri), but no recent history of structural conflict between them. Rather, it is the history of the past that looms large (for example, the unequal treaties).

All this is complex material out of which almost anything can be wrought, from very friendly cooperation to bitter conflict. Take the famous "three obstacles" China has indicated as standing in the way of good relations with the Soviet Union: the Soviet invasion of Afghanistan, the Vietnam invasion of Kampuchea, and the Soviet troops stationed in Mongolia. The highly dynamic Gorbachev regime will probably make it possible to remove all three within the coming three to five years. But are we really to believe that this is all? What about the intense competition between countries trying in similar ways to graft capitalist principles onto a socialist formation? Would that not be like the competition among countries (successfully) grafting socialist principles onto a capitalist formation? Like Japan and the mini-Japans / Chinas, not only having an ambiguous relationship, but possibly also being on a collision course?

Further complicating the matter is the complexity of the internal dynamism. We are dealing with countries in the Pacific hemisphere struggling at the same time with all three social formations: feudalism, capitalism, and socialism. Latin America and the Philippines, just to take two examples, are obviously struggling with the shackles of feudalism, the heavy burden resting on those societies because of the position of *los poderes fácticos*—the church, the landowners/*latifundistas,* the military—which then ally themselves with the burgeoning class of big and small business people, in turn usually the allies of foreign business people from big, important countries like the United States and Japan. To liberate a country from *los poderes fácticos* is to free it from the shackles of feudalism; a necessary condition for both democracy and development.

But if that happens, the experience is that the shackles of capitalism are not far away. National and foreign business take over as the leading powers in society, and as a result massive exploitation sets in. Economic growth will come, together with its close relative, economic inequality, pushing some people into incredible wealth and others, a considerably more numerous group, into equally incredible misery. Where feudalism was exploitative and familistic, capitalism is exploitative and mercilessly contractual. Both of them have strong coercive elements. At the same time, nature will be squandered and used for purposes very far removed from the satisfaction of basic human needs, a factor which will then contribute even further to the misery.

To get rid of these conditions is to get rid of the shackles of capitalism. But the moment that is done the shackles of socialism are usually not very far away. They usually take the form of a heavy-handed state bureaucracy, engaged in detailed planning, stifling free entrepreneurship and competition and risk-willing capital, getting people out of misery from below, and then landing everybody, from all corners of society, in generalized, gray poverty. In this situation neither capital, nor technology for supplying consumer goods, nor good management is likely to be easily available. Nature in the sense of land and raw materials will be liberated from private ownership. But the state or communal ownership that takes over will not have the necessary capital, technology, or management skills to bear upon it. And people are unfree, neither permitted nor willing to take risks.

So those are the problems of shaking off the shackles of socialism: liberate capital again, get research and technology going also in the field of consumer goods, and develop adequate management practices. And all of this should be done without falling into the hands of whatever vestiges there might be of feudal and capitalist social formations—and without re-creating them. One interesting point in that connection is that we have no basis for guessing the future since we are essentially entering virgin social history. We are at the edge of history. And that edge of history is not located in Europe, nor in the Americas. It is located in East Asia, above all in China and the Soviet Union, and perhaps in the potentially most dynamic part of the Soviet Union, the one bordering on the Pacific, home to between a quarter and a third of humanity. Echoes of these two giant experiments will be found in Socialist East Asia and in Socialist Europe—and everywhere else for that matter.

Going back to Table 3: Are there some conclusions that can be drawn? The advantage of a table like this is that it makes possible a transition from the conventional analysis of conflict in terms of bilateral relations between two actors at a time to a more wholistic approach. To facilitate the latter there is a column at the far right in the table in which are added up the numbers of negative and positive relations. Again, it should be emphasized how subjective this judgment is and also how noncomparable many of the conflicts are. Adding them up, meaning giving equal weight to each of them, is hazardous to say the least.

And yet we get some gross information from the table. Thus, both the United States and Japan have managed to score a full house where negative relations are concerned: 10. No doubt there is a major difference. Japan's experience with direct violence is of the past, but on the other hand it was atrocious. The U.S. relation to direct violence is in the present and possibly in the future, the general idea being that the United States came as a liberator during the Pacific war. The U.S. approach is through military bases and military preparedness; that is not (yet) the Japanese approach. When it comes to structural violence they are perhaps more comparable, with the United States more repressive and Japan more exploitative.[10]

In other words, in adding up and comparing past and present, a moral equivalence is more or less implicitly assumed to the effect that present preparedness (basically with nuclear arms) is seen as the equivalent of past atrocities. For that reason the Soviet Union also comes high up. But since so many of the Soviet relationships in the Pacific hemisphere are vacuous, the score, 6, is shared with many actors: China, mini-Japans/Chinas, Southeast Asia, New Zealand/Australia. The latter two, however, cancel this to some extent with many positive relations in the area, although not quite up to the level of the most positively inserted actor of them all: Canada.

It will be noted that in saying all of this no distinction is made between being an initiator of a conflict, the subject so to speak, and the object. Being party to a conflict is what counts here. Nevertheless, based on this general image of the situation, let us try to draw some tentative conclusions.

First, if the policies of the United States and Japan in the Pacific could improve, that would help considerably since these two countries alone account for much more than their fair share of the total conflict material. As a matter of fact, Japan could reduce her share in a very simple manner as the eight direct conflicts relate to the past. That past is now being re-lived through the statements occasionally coming from high levels in Japan, the textbook revision by the Ministry of Education being only one example. Nobody with a sense of history would demand of Japan that the country should assume 100% responsibility for what happened. But it is a far step from that stand to 0%, indicating that not only was the Pacific war "war as normal," it was also "politics as normal" and essentially the consequence of causes located in the West (colonization of East Asia).[11]

The psychological processing of the war that was is almost as important as the preparedness for the war that could come. And where that is concerned, the provocative, offensive military doctrine underlying U.S. foreign policy is almost as important as the concrete preparedness for the possible next war. Since this affects seven of the ten negative points for the United States, the relationships with South America, the Pacific Islands, New Zealand/Australia, Southeast Asia (particularly the Philippines), the mini-Japans/Chinas (particularly South Korea) the relationship with Japan, and indeed the relationship with the Soviet Union, a change in military doctrine to defense of the United States, rather than military presence practically everywhere, would be significant. Also significant would be a more adequate processing of what the United States did to Socialist East Asia, and not only to the Indochina countries but also to Korea. In the United States there is not even anything to revise, there never having been a real admission of basic responsibility for what happened except in the sense of the second Indochina War being a "tragic mistake."

Of course, any change in military doctrine from offensive defense to defensive defense would have to be negotiated with the Soviet Union. Interestingly enough, that kind of change is at least debated inside the Soviet Union, in high circles.[12] In the United States it still remains a taboo area, even to the point that the most elementary thinking underlying this kind of change seems not to emerge, at least not for the time being.

Having said this, at least a very partial answer is given to a rather important question: If we remove not two actors, but the most objectionable aspects of their policies, what would come in their place? Is there, at the more wholistic level, some kind of system balance that would have to be reestablished? In other words, if Japan and the United States assumed responsibility for their belligerence of the past, up to a level reasonably compatible with what reasonably objective historians might arrive at, would another country emerge with equally self-righteous and aggressive doctrines instead? Not impossible. There may be some kind of balance at the structural level of which we are not aware because our perspective is not sufficiently macro, either in time or in space. But off-hand it sounds relatively unlikely.

What is considerably less unlikely is that a retooling of the two superpowers toward a more defensive military doctrine might leave the field open for somebody else who would like to retool in the opposite direction. Japan? China? The Pacific Ocean for the Asians (as opposed to the Pacific Islanders)? There are several possibilities. All of them point in the same direction: the need for a Pacific Hemisphere Peace Conference, initiating a new approach in the entire area.

And that, of course, focuses interest on one glaring and rather eloquent actor missing in this discussion of the Pacific hemisphere: a Pacific Hemisphere Forum worthy of its name, bringing together all the actors mentioned above, with no hegemonial assumption entertained by anybody, like the South Pacific Forum, only much more comprehensive. Sooner or later that will have to emerge in order to handle the intricacies of direct and structural violence, of military and economic matters, and the underlying cultural assumptions. The setting has to provide sufficient political articulation to make all these issues debatable even if solutions of problems and conflicts are not around the corner. Here again the table might be a guide as to who should take the initiative. The obvious candidate would be the country with the highest positive scores: Canada on the eastern rim of the Pacific, Japan on the western rim, and New Zealand/Australia from the Pacific Islands. East and West, capitalist and socialist together, they could constitute an important factor for a future of peace in the area.

But that future is certainly not yet here. There are some rather difficult intermediate steps. One such step has already been indicated above. The omnipresence of the U.S. military machine would probably have to be reduced considerably even in the near future, if for no other reason than simple economic considerations. Bases will have to be eliminated. One negative implication of this will in all likelihood be felt in the "hub" of the Pacific, Hawaii. Any withdrawal of U.S. military presence in the south, the southeast, and the east will probably be accompanied by a heavy concentration of military capability in the Hawaiian archipelago for rapid deployment "should the need arise." This possibility should be anticipated and if at all possible negated in advance, since whatever would be gained through partial withdrawal (such as closing the base complex in the Philippines in return for the Soviet Union closing the bases in Vietnam) might be canceled.

And that leads me to the final point to be considered: the native peoples in the Pacific hemisphere. They are all over the place, as is logical given the circumstance that the whites have arrived relatively recently. There are also native peoples in Japan and China and other places, again natural given the circumstance that they were the inhabitants before what today is counted as "the Japanese" and "the Chinese" were solidly established.

But what does this have to do with international affairs? Increasingly much, and for the above-mentioned reason: the actors in the area will more and more be evaluated in terms of the way they treat native peoples. The United States will be seen in terms of its relationship with Native Americans in general and native Hawaiians (Polynesians) in particular. The same will apply to Canada. And the same will certainly apply to the Iberic regimes on the Pacific coast of South America, to Mexico and Central America, Colombia, Ecuador, Peru, Bolivia, Chile. They will all be seen in terms of what happens to the Native Americans, *"los indios."* In New Zealand/Australia this is already clear: New Zealand fares much better internationally precisely because the Maoris today seem to stand a better chance than the "Aborigines" in Australia.

As mentioned, on the western rim of the Pacific this *problematique* is less developed because it is not expressed in terms of whites versus colored. But Japan and China should not rest convinced that the Ainus and the non-Han peoples and their fate are unknown elsewhere. Moreover, however much the Soviet Union may be rightly criticized for not granting native peoples much in terms of civil and political rights, the economic and cultural rights are better taken care of. This may give the country a certain edge internationally even though the native focus will increasingly be on sharing political (and military) power.

Hence, let us add mentally a last column to the right in Table 3:

the internal situation, precisely relative to native Pacific peoples. A new arena of international politics emerges: a possible race for the future, trying to gain points in international standing by reversing some of the terrible patterns of direct and structural violence these peoples have been exposed to. Needless to say, the actor not included in the map but yet important, France, fares extremely badly precisely on this dimension, in addition to the nuclear way in which that absentee landlord has inserted itself in the region.

In short, there is more than enough for a Pacific Hemisphere Forum to discuss. Much of this can be done in the United Nations, and should be done under the aegis of the United Nations. But it could also be done in the Pacific hemisphere itself. More precisely, in Hawaii, thereby underlining that the archipelago is considerably more than one of fifty states in what is still the most powerful actor in the region. And one day the United States might come to the conclusion that a pacific Pacific is in the U.S. interest, even to the point of encouraging Hawaii to become the Geneva of the Pacific.

NOTES

CHAPTER 1

1. No. 9, 1979. See also J. Galtung and T. Höivik, in J. Galtung, *Essays in Peace Research,* vol. I (Copenhagen: Ejlers, 1975), chapter 5.

2. Quincy Wright, *A Study of War* (Chicago: University of Chicago Press, 1942). See also J. Galtung and T. Broch, "Belligerence Among the Primitives," in J. Galtung, *Essays in Peace Research,* vol. II (1977), chapter 1.

3. *Journal of Peace Research,* 1978, no. 3, pp. 227–241.

4. Published annually from World Priorities, Box 25140, Washington, D.C.

5. According to General John A. Wickham, Jr., in an R.O.T.C. lecture at Princeton University, 26 February 1987.

6. See J. Galtung and A. Preiswerk, eds., *Self-Reliance* (London: Bougle d'Ouverture, 1980).

CHAPTER 2 and ADDENDUM

1. There is a peculiar symmetry in the world. There are two major oceans defining the Atlantic and Pacific theaters, separated by the Americas on the one hand, and by an enormous landmass that can be described as the Soviet Union with Europe (West and East) on top; in the middle, Asia (West, South, Southeast, and East); and at the bottom, Africa. The North became stronger and more expansionist for a number of reasons (climate, missionary Christianity with its secular offsprings liberalism/conservatism-capitalism and marxism-socialism). Only the United States and the Soviet Union, the two superpowers, border on both oceans and can be superactive in both theaters; in that sense they are both global powers although the U.S. deployment and networks in general are more far-reaching. Geopolitically the Americas "belong to" the United States and Eurasia to the Soviet Union (and nobody bothers much about Africa). This position is contested by the U.S. bridgeheads in Western Europe and Southeast/East Asia and the Soviet bridgehead in Cuba (not to mention the U.S. fear of more bridgeheads). But this is a "geopolitical" vision—a perspective that can best be identified as some kind of global fascism, that implies that geo, the world, is up for bidding and belongs to the stronger, singly or in concert.

2. The British historian A. J. P. Taylor puts it as follows: "As Stalin said later,

accurately summing up the record of war, 'Great Britain provided time; the United States provided money and Soviet Russia provided blood' " (*Essays in English History*, London: Penguin, 1976, p. 298). The figures are official Soviet figures, quoted by Stephen Cohen in several articles (such as *The Nation*, 26 January 1985, p.72).

3. In July 1945 there were other concerns in China. After all, the victory of Mao Zedong's forces, as we know in retrospect, was little more than four years away.

4. A basic reason why the International Military Tribunal for the Far East verdict is more problematic than that of the Nürnberg Tribunal. It is hard to imagine a dissent so fundamental as that of the Indian Judge Pal (or perhaps of the Dutch Judge Röling) in the Nürnberg case. The culprits stood out so clearly. But then there is certainly also the problem of using law retroactively, and of the moral status of the victors—the latter particularly in a Far East context against a background of highly violent U.S., British, French (and Dutch, for that matter) colonialism. For an excellent description both of the degree of consensus and of the little there was of resistance in Japan, see Ienaga Saburo, *The Pacific War 1931-1945* (New York: Pantheon Books, 1978), particularly chapter 10, "Dissent and Resistance."

5. How does one explain this? It defies the explanatory power of any social science I know of, at least. On the other hand, although the United States forces had to withdraw, they left behind, cruelly, two time bombs with a devastating impact on Vietnam: an ecocide with genocidal consequences, and heavy militarization of a relatively small country. So, who won?

6. See my article "Goals and Processes in Spanish Politics; Western Incorporation or Autonomy," chapter 12 in *Essays in Peace Research*, vol. 6 (1988).

7. And the corresponding idea, frequently held by the elite, would be that the people on the other side are good, for they must be the enemy of the enemy of my friend! Thus, the governments of Western European countries seem firmly convinced that people in Eastern Europe agree with them rather than with their own governments where foreign affairs are concerned. However, public opinion research may reveal something else: the views of foreign affairs are rather in line with official policies in general terms if not necessarily on very specific events. See H. Ornauer, A. Sicinski, H. Wiberg, and J. Galtung, eds., *Images of the World in the Year 2000* (The Hague: Mouton, 1976), Conclusion.

8. And by guerrillas not in power. Japan could not capitulate to Korean guerrillas.

9. Thus, RimPac exercises involved the United States, Australia, New Zealand—in other words, ANZUS—and Canada from 1971, and Japan was requested to participate by the Carter administration and did so. "For Japan to take part in the exercise alongside nations with which Japan had no security treaty was deemed by many to be illegal"—as pointed out by Takita Kenji, "The Emerging Geopolitical Situation and Changing Pattern of Reactions to it in the Asia-Pacific Region," paper presented at the 27th Annual Meeting of the International Studies Association, Anaheim, California, March 25-29, 1986. AMPO, incidentally, stands for *Nichibei Anzen Hosho Joyaku*, Japan–U.S. Security Treaty.

10. That gives us a total of three analytical perspectives: the predetermination of the configuration by the Second World War; internal development inside the alliances; and the *actio-reactio* system between the two alliances.

11. To illustrate this, the thick broken lines in Figure 1 would be within the circles/countries, between elites and people, and particularly in the periphery rather

than between countries. One could then imagine all kinds of shades in between purely intra-country and purely inter-country dominated conflict formations.

12. For a very creative approach to the Korean impasse, see Glenn Paige, "Nonviolent Global Transformation and Peaceful Korean Reunification" (University of Hawaii, Dept. of Political Science, July 1985).

My own point would be that a generational shift is needed in both Koreas, and that will come in the 1990s when new generations have come into power (after forty years?). The four Kuril islands may be a part of a major economic deal between Japan and the Soviet Union over Siberia.

13. For an effort to use a Chinese sense of dialectics as an explanatory principle for Chinese politics, see my "Chinese Strategy of Development, A Contribution to an Everlasting Debate," in Sung-Jo Park, *The 21st-Century, The Asian Century?* (Berlin: Express, 1985), pp. 43–58.

14. On the other hand, the Western tendency to emphasize the bilateral nature of Soviet relations to Eastern European countries as opposed to the multilateralism of the West may be a carry-over from the Stalin period in the East and the West. More probably WTO has had a moderating influence on the Soviet Union.

15. This was the "socialist world" when Hitler attacked in June 1941: the Soviet Union and Mongolia. Ten years later it was a good third of humanity, from the Elbe to the Japan/China sea—with both East and West expecting that socialism would extend farther, in all directions. Twenty years later the socialist world was still in disarray with the Soviet Union failing to keep the flock together—and that has been the situation ever since. Now even socialism as an ideology is in total disarray.

16. But was it an intervention or an effort to stave off an intervention by a nationalist Polish general? In that case, what is the difference if the threat of intervention is so credible that a military coup is the response?

17. No doubt Prime Minister Lange, who is also minister in the sense of being a lay Methodist preacher, will stand out in history as the first statesman in one of the alliance systems with sufficient courage to challenge nuclearism.

18. This was the logic in which Spain was caught by the UCD government that joined the alliance, and by the PSOE government under González that, I presume, originally had the intention of leaving or at least seriously contesting the membership.

19. Again, Spain may be an example. The military may have been able to put the problematique in terms of "less nuclearism, but then membership" versus "no membership, but then nuclearism—under France, if not under the United States." González steered the referendum of March 1986 toward the former and probably wants both.

20. Rumania's nationally independent, militia type defense forces are, of course, seen by the Soviet Union as a vote of distrust, as being a defensive capability to deter Soviet rather than "imperialist" or "revanchist" attack. If the United States threatens not to buy butter from a recalcitrant New Zealand, would it not stand to reason that the Soviet Union might force Rumania to pay an economic price for their acts of defiance, inspired, originally, by the Soviet intervention in Hungary?

21. And they would, of course, be very sensitive to the expressions of protest: not so much doubts about weapons of mass destruction such as nuclear systems, but proposals to build independent defense systems, be that with offensive arms including

independent nuclear forces (France, England) or with defensive arms now being con-
templated by nuclear unilateralists both in SPD in Germany, the Labour Party in
England, and to some extent by the PCI in Italy.

22. I mean by "South America" all countries to the south of North America, starting with Mexico, avoiding the name of the conquerors ("Latin").

23. For an early publication in the field of relationship between provision of training and advice in the military sector and demand for arms, see Geoffrey Kemp, *Some
Relationships between U.S. Military Training in Latin America and Weapons Acqui-
sition Patterns: 1959-1969* (Cambridge, Mass.: Center for International Studies,
MIT, 1970). For a much more analytical exploration, see Malvern Lumsden, "The
Role of the Military in the World Economic Order: Perspectives for Peace and Development Research," paper presented at the Seventh Nordic Peace Research Conference, Silkeborg, Denmark, 1976.

24. This is a basic thesis of my book *There Are Alternatives!* (Nottingham:
Spokesman, 1984)—also in Norwegian, Swedish, Dutch, German, Italian, Spanish,
and Japanese editions. (See note 27, below.)

25. Sometimes one may wonder whether NATO and WTO really exist or are just
creations in the minds of some skillful public relations managers. Thus, does it really
stand to reason that the elites in these countries will follow their superpowers into
military adventures that cannot unambiguously be seen as caused by an unprovoked
attack from the other side? And is it ever likely that any situation will be that unam-
biguous?

26. I think this term was first used by the late Sugata Dasgupta in his paper at the
Second IPRA Conference, Tallberg, Sweden, June 1967, together with the term
maldevelopment—to articulate the point that peacelessness is some kind of peace, it
is not war; and maldevelopment is also some kind of development, it is not status
quo. And yet the one is not peace, and the other is not development.

27. Nottingham: Spokesman, 1984; Wiesbaden: Westdeutscher Verlag, 1984;
Madrid: Editorial Tecnos, 1984; Amersfoort: de Horstink, 1984; Stockholm: Gid-
lunds, 1985; Oslo: FMK-PAX, 1985; Torino: Abele, 1986, and Tokyo: Keiso Shobo,
1989.

28. See *There Are Alternatives!*, chapter 5.2, for a discussion of the distinction
between defensive and offensive weapons systems, based on the range of delivery and
the area of destruction. The distinction is certainly not sharp, but sharper than the
distinction between offensive weapons systems for first or second strike.

29. Particularly significant in this connection for some time was the fisheries'
agreement between Vanuatu and the Soviet Union.

30. Territorial small in terms of size, demographically small in terms of population, politically small in terms of autonomy—often all three combined. An example
is Palau/Belau; see *From Trusteeship to—? Micronesia and Its Future,* Pacific Concerns Resource Center, Honolulu, July 1982.

31. I am thinking of what may happen in the wake of the reorientation of Soviet
policy in the "Far East" after Gorbachev's Vladivostok speech in July 1986.

32. For a country with a self-image of that kind to insert itself in the world of bilateral and multilateral interaction must be quite problematic.

33. U.S. pressure seems so far (1988) to have been more rhetorical than real—
except for the tension in ANZUS, of course. As late as December 1986 (the ban of

U.S. nuclear-capable ships from New Zealand's ports dates from February 1985), U.S. Navy Secretary John Lehman called for U.S. economic sanctions against New Zealand (*Japan Times,* 17 December 1986). On the other hand, "New Zealand will remain in the Five-Power Defense Arrangement (FPDA) involving Britain, Australia, New Zealand, Malaysia and Singapore." (*Japan Times,* 24 December 1986.)

34. For a good example of a sober analysis of the Soviet Union, see Mohamed Noordin Sopiee, *The Russian Threat: Between Alarm and Complacency* (Malaysia: ISIS, 1985). The opening words are: "We used to be told by many Americans that China was a grave threat. Now we are being told by as many Americans that the Soviet Union is a grave threat and that China is no threat at all." Also see his "Approaches to Peace and Economic Co-operation in Southeast Asia," in H. Matsumoto and N. Sopiee, eds., *Into the Pacific Era, Southeast Asia and Its Place in the Pacific* (Malaysia: ISIS, 1986), pp. 15–24.

35. Operationalized as a score of 96 in Table 2.

CHAPTER 3

1. See Saburo Ienaga, *The Pacific War 1913–1945* (New York: Random House, 1978), particularly chapter 9, "The Horrors of War," pp. 181–202. According to Ienaga, "military deaths in combat from the start of the war in China totaled 2.3 million" (p. 197).

2. See J. Galtung, "The Basic Human Needs Approach," in K. Lederer, et al., *Basic Human Needs: A Contribution to the Current Debate* (Konigstein: Hain, 1980).

3. Hitler had his program, to make not only Germany but Europe *Judenrein.* Stalin had his, *Kulakrein.* The present leadership of Israel (1988) seems to be heading for *Arabrein* as the basic policy for Greater Israel. And the United States has for a long time had a combination of containment and *Kommunistenrein* as two basic guidelines, with elements of coexistence.

4. See J. Galtung, *United States Foreign Policy as Manifest Theology* Institute on Global Conflict and Cooperation, University of California at San Diego, 1987.

5. See J. Galtung, "The Real Star Wars Threat," *The Nation,* 28 February 1987, pp. 248–49. According to *Samoa News,* 2 February 1988, Star Wars "testing in the Pacific currently is conducted atop the extinct volcano Haleakala on the Hawaiian island of Maui," and "Wake Island is to be the next 'Star Wars' base in the Pacific Ocean, according to an Army report."

The United States is probably far closer than the Soviet Union to any kind of deployment; the Soviet Union possibly focusing on the capability to destroy whatever capability the United States may have in this field. This relationship—the United States taking on a more aggressive and the Soviet Union a more defensive stance—is certainly also found in the pre Star Wars deployment pattern with the United States deployment being in terms of very forward basing close to the Soviet Union in Japan, South Korea, Okinawa, Guam, and the Subic Bay/Clark Field complex in the Philippines, as opposed to the lonely Soviet base in Vietnam (Cam Ranh Bay), and no base close to United States territory except in the Bering strait. See *The Economist,* 14 November 1987, p. 41, for one survey of the situation. The missile tests, however, reach the Mid-Pacific from both the Soviet Union and the United States, and from China. And then there are the ongoing French nuclear explosions in Moruroa. For the best exposure of "how the nuclear build-up in the cause of 'peace' fuels the threat of war," see Peter Hayes et al., *American Lake, Nuclear Peril in the Pacific* (Ringwood, Australia: Penguin Books, 1986). For the Australian case, see J. A. Camilleri, *ANZUS, Australia's Predicament in the Nuclear Age* (Melbourne: Macmillan, 1987).

6. An example would be Chile, sometimes referring to itself as *el ultimo rincon del mundo,* the last corner of the world. But even the last corner seems to feel good by having something even further out (or up, the general relationship to Bolivia).

7. I would certainly argue that the effort is successfully continued with the present Japanese economic penetration of Australia.

8. The wording he used at a talk in Honolulu on 19 October 1987 was, "New Zealand's perspectives are increasingly shaped by the reality of our location. We now not only accept, but celebrate, what the map tells us—that we are a South Pacific nation" (*Ka Leo o Hawaii,* 28 October 1987, p. 5). It all started with Lange personally denying the U.S.S. *Buchanan* port access on 4 February 1985. His administration inherited a situation where security was seen as military, he said, and posited against this a set of five principles that certainly may serve as guidelines for peace and development in the whole area: (1) implement a comprehensive security policy, all aspects, (2) have this include the use of resources, (3) honor the South Pacific Nuclear Free Zone policy, from Raratonga in 1985, not accepted by the United States, (4) be very deliberate about this, "we knew what we did," and (5) do so not out of anti-Americanism but as making a stand against nuclear weapons. It should be pointed out that this is not an antimilitary policy in general as "New Zealand will remain in the Five-Power Defense Arrangement (FPDA) involving Britain, Australia, New Zealand, Malaysia and Sigapore" (*Japan Times,* 24 December 1986). But the New Zealand Singapore-based infantry battalion will be withdrawn in 1989. Lange was given the Distinguished Peace Leadership Award of the Nuclear Age Peace Foundation for 1988 in Santa Barbara, California.

9. Socialist countries, however, have traditionally been more open to developing their human resources, through health and education if not so much in terms of individual liberties, as in developing their natural resources through good environmental policies.

10. As an example of United States repressive tactics may serve the policy in Palau/Belau. The Japanese, of course, were very repressive during the Pacific war. It should be noted that it is very possible to be one without the other; exploitation and repression are two different faces of structural violence.

11. One example would be the statement by Japan's then National Land Agency director, Seisuke Okuno, that Japan fought in the war "to protect itself when the white race had turned Asia into a colony," as reported in *Honolulu Advertiser,* 28 April 1988. That this is one side of a multifaceted truth is obvious; but it is remarkable how difficult it is to articulate more than one side at a time.

12. Mikhail Gorbachev in "The Realities and Guarantees of a Secure World," *Pravda,* 17 September 1987: "These notions presuppose such a structure of the armed forces of a state that they would be sufficient to repulse a possible aggression but would not be sufficient for the conduct of offensive actions."